Hush No More

VANESSA DUNN GUYTON

No part of this publication may be reproduced or transmitted in any form or by any means, electronic or mechanical, including photocopy, recording, or any information from the publisher, except for brief quotations used in critical articles and reviews.

Printed in the United States of America Copyright © Vanessa Dunn Guyton, 2019 All Rights Reserved

Published by Consulting Experts & Associates, 261 Business Park Blvd., Columbia, SC 29229

The information in this book is designed to both provide helpful information on the subjects discussed and motivate readers to action. This book is not meant to be used as a tool to diagnose or treat any psychological condition. It is sold with the understanding that the authors and publisher are not engaged to render any type of psychological, legal, or any other kind of professional advice. The content is the sole expression and opinion of its authors. Neither the publisher nor the authors shall be liable for any physical, psychological, emotional, financial, or commercial damages incurred as a result of this text. You are responsible for your own choices, actions, and results. Only you can make the life you want.

ACKNOWLEDGEMENTS

A big thank-you goes to our amazing Creator and to my parents, Freddie and Geneva Dunn. I promise to continue making you proud by being a positive force for good in this world.

My heart will always be held by my children, Keith, Teaira, Tony, Miata, and De'Quan, as well as my grandchildren, Braylin and Jeremiah. As I work to build our legacy, I hope to forever remain an example and an inspiration for you all.

I owe many of my successes in large part to my amazing Life and Success Strategist Coach, Angela Carr Patterson. Your guidance, patience, gifts, and wisdom have contributed significantly to the 'HUSH No More' book, documentary, and movement. For that, I will always be grateful and thankful to have you in my life.

A special thank-you to all my friends who have helped me through my trauma by listening to me and actively supporting me: Angela, Shai, CJ, Valerie, Tasha, Erica, Dean, and Tony.

To the man who raped me, I want you to know that your actions did not break me, but rather motivated me to change the world and create a heightened awareness that leads to prevention.

DEDICATION

This project is dedicated to the authors of this book for your courage and strength to overcome your trauma, and your willingness to help others by deciding that you will HUSH No More because YOU HAVE A RIGHT TO TELL IT.

Additionally, to all past and future victims of the HUSH topics who find their voice and courage to become survivors, may this book serve as a reminder that you are not alone, and you have a right to tell it!

Table of Contents

Introduction/Purpose 1

Definitions 3

Research/National Statistics 10

Effects of The Hush Topics 17

False Reports 19

Our Right to Tell It 22

Domestic Violence 23

    BUT I LOVE YOU! 25

    My Father, My Hero 27

    The Color of Love 34

    Get Mad 35

Sexual Assault 40

    I Trusted You Intro 40

    Hush No More 51

    My Temple 58

    My Thoughts During the Winter of 2013 62

    Speak Up 63

Child Sexual Abuse 70

Freddy Krueger 70

Between Sisters 75

Finding Purpose in the Pain 76

Molestation and Manipulation 90

Sexual Harassment 105

Exposed 105

Sex Trafficking 112

Superstar 112

Dr. Guyton's Right to Tell It 123

R. Kelly 123

When a Date Turns to Rape 125

Support/ Words of Encouragement 147

Survivor's Pledge 148

A Meditation for Survivors 149

Friends & Family Support 153

Support Hotline Numbers 156

About the Author 157

Introduction/Purpose

The HUSH No More Movement was created to elevate awareness of the negative impacts that sexual assault, sexual harassment, domestic violence, sex trafficking, and other violent crimes have had on the lives of victims. This is a rapidly growing movement to bring awareness that will lead to the prevention and ultimate end of all those aforementioned horrible acts. Our goal here is to provide an active. outlet for survivors to share their stories of pain, betrayal, abuse, and most important, growth By sharing the stories of some fearless survivors who dared to stand tall and share their truth, we hope to inspire others to muster the strength to overcome all the social stigmas and shame, survive, and thrive with the incredible resilience of love and forgiveness.

Each year millions of individuals fall victim to heinous sexual crimes and domestic violence that often goes unreported. These victims, young and old, male and female, of every race and background, frequently go years without telling anyone of the trauma they have experienced at the hands of their perpetrators.

Many have taken their pain to their graves while many others live among us, work with us, pray with us, and walk by us every day without as much as a whisper about the hell they are experiencing in their lives.

Some fear their perpetrators and abusers, others hold a fear of shame, and many simply fear not being believed.

While this gripping fear has silenced many of their voices, now we are encouraging victims to become survivors by Helping Unleash the Shame to Heal and providing advocacy services and training that hopefully lead to the prevention of all the HUSH Topics.

Definitions

HUSH Topics: HUSH Topics are those topics that individuals, families, and organizations have a hard time discussing, such as sexual assault, domestic violence, child sexual abuse, sex trafficking, sexual harassment, etc.

Survivor: A person who can cope and grow after suffering a traumatic event.

Victim: A person harmed, injured, or killed as a result of a crime. A person harmed or injured may still be suffering and wounded mentally and/or physically.

Victimology: The study of the victims of crime and the psychological effects caused by their traumatic experiences.

Source: Webster's Dictionary

Domestic violence: Domestic violence is an intentional pattern of physical, emotional, economic, sexual, and other tactics to instill fear and to coerce intimate partners to act against their own will or best interests. The behavior can be subtle with abusers using a variety of ways to gain control, including insulting their partners, controlling their contact with family members and friends, and/

or limiting how their partners can spend money. Abuse can worsen and become more frequent with consistent physical injuries, such as hitting or slapping, sexual assaults, or threats to their partner's safety.

5 Types of Domestic Abuse

Emotional abuse: Emotional abuse is almost like brainwashing in that it is done to wear away at a victim's self-confidence. It can be verbal abuse, such as your partner repeatedly criticizing, intimidating, or belittling you. It can also be nonverbal abuse, or coercive control, when your partner asserts control and tries to demean you by making decisions on your behalf. This can include anything from what you should wear to who your friends should be.

Financial abuse: This type of abuse involves stealing or withholding money from the victim or using the victim's name and personal information to accrue debt. The victim may feel financially dependent on their partner to the point where they feel obligated to be submissive, or as though they are being forced to support their partner financially.

Physical abuse: This is the use of physical force against another person to inflict injury or put the person at risk of becoming injured. This may include your partner pushing, hitting, choking, or threatening you with a weapon.

Sexual abuse: This abuse often occurs in tandem with physical abuse. It involves forcing or coercing a victim to do something sexually, which can range from unwanted kissing or touching to rape. This can also involve threatening someone to perform a sexual act including oral sex, restricting a victim's access to birth control and condoms, or repeatedly using sexual insults to demean a victim.

Spiritual abuse: It is also referred to as religious abuse. This involves a partner not allowing you to practice your moral or religious beliefs. It can include humiliation or harassment as a means of control, forcing a victim to give up their culture or values that are important to them. Spiritual abuse can be used by religious leaders to instill fear or guilt into a victim, coercing them to behave a certain way.

Source: Domesticshelters.org

Intimate partner violence: Societal perspectives have expanded to understand better the types of violence that exist within relationships as well as the reality that the roles of abuser and victim are not gender- specific. As a result, the term "intimate partner violence" has been introduced to encompass a broader understanding of violence in relationships.

The concept of intimate partner violence acknowledges that abuse can exist in any intimate relationship, regardless of sexual orientation, marital status, or gender. Like "domestic violence," this new term does not confine the roles of abuser and victim to just one gender.

Source: https://inpublicsafety.com/2015/10/domestic-violence-and-intimate-partner-violence-whats-the-difference/

Sexual assault: This term refers to unwanted sexual acts against or without a person's consent. This includes any sexual, physical, verbal, or visual act that forces a person to engage in sexual contact against their will or without their consent. Sexual assault and rape may sometimes overlap and be used interchangeably in some circumstances. However, it is best to consult laws set at the state level to determine the exact difference between the two as this may vary depending on the jurisdiction.

Source: Raiin.org

Rape: The penetration, no matter how slight, of the vagina or anus with any body part, object, or oral penetration by a sex organ of another person without the consent of the victim. This definition includes any gender of victim and perpetrator, not just women being raped by men. It also recognizes that rape with an object can be as traumatic as penile/vaginal rape. This definition also includes instances in which the victim is unable to give consent because of temporary or permanent mental or physical incapacity. Furthermore, because many rapes are facilitated by drugs or alcohol, the new definition recognizes that a victim can be incapacitated and thus unable to consent because of ingestion of drugs or alcohol. Similarly, a victim may be legally incapable of consent because of age. The ability of the victim to give consent must be determined by the state statutes. Physical resistance is not required on the part of the victim to demonstrate lack of consent.

Source: Department of Justice

Sexual harassment: Repeated uninvited contact (verbal, physical, or otherwise) against another person, like an applicant or an employee, of a sexual nature falls under the category of sexual harassment. This is defined as any unwelcome sexual advances, requests for sexual favors, and other verbal or physical harassment of a sexual form.

Visit https://www.eeoc.gov/employees/howtofile.cfm to file a complaint against an employer for discrimination, including discrimination as a result of your unwillingness to perform any sexual favors or stay quiet in the face of sexual harassment. Complaints can be filed online, in person, or via mail. Individuals have 180 days to file a claim.

Source: Equal Employment Opportunity Commission (EEOC)

Child sexual abuse: Child sexual abuse is a form of child abuse that includes sexual activity with a minor. A child cannot consent to any form of sexual activity, period. When a perpetrator engages with a child this way, they are committing a crime that can have long-lasting effects on the victim. Child sexual abuse does not need to include physical contact between a perpetrator and a child. Some forms of child sexual abuse include:

- Exhibitionism, or exposing oneself to a minor
- Fondling
- Intercourse
- Masturbation in the presence of a minor or forcing the minor to masturbate
- Obscene phone calls, text messages, or digital interactions
- Producing, owning, or sharing pornographic images or movies of children
- Sex of any kind with a minor, including vaginal, oral, or anal
- Sex trafficking
- Any other sexual conduct that is harmful to a child's mental, emotional, or physical welfare

Child abuse perpetrator: A perpetrator does not have to be an adult to harm a child. They can have any relationship with the child including an older sibling, playmate, family member, teacher, coach, neighbor, instructor, caretaker, or parent of another child.

The majority of perpetrators are someone the child or family knows. We highly recommend that parents be careful about who is allowed to spend time unsupervised with their children.

Source: Rainn.org

Sex trafficking: Sex trafficking is a form of modern-day slavery in which individuals perform commercial sex through the use of force, fraud, or coercion. Minors under the age of eighteen engaging in commercial sex are considered to be victims of human trafficking, regardless of the use of force, fraud, or coercion. Sex trafficking often takes the form of escort services, nonconsensual pornographies, illicit massage businesses, brothels, and the outdoor solicitation of prostitution or any services of a sexual nature.

Source: polarisproject.org

Research/National Statistics

The statistics below are based on surveys conducted by the Department of Justice and other nonprofit organizations. However, experts estimate that there are many more victims who go uncounted because they have not come forward to report their traumatic experiences from one or more of the HUSH Topics.

Domestic/Intimate Partner Violence:

- On average, nearly 20 people per minute are physically abused by an intimate partner in the United States. For one year, this equates to more than 10 million women and men.
    - 1 in 3 women and 1 in 4 men have experienced some form of physical violence by an intimate partner.
    - 1 in 7 women and 1 in 25 men have been injured by an intimate partner.
    - 1 in 10 women have been raped by an intimate partner. Accurate data for male victims was unavailable at the time of writing.
- 1 in 4 women and 1 in 7 men have been victims of severe physical violence (e.g., beating, burning, strangling) by an intimate partner in their lifetime.

- 1 in 7 women and 1 in 18 men have been stalked by an intimate partner during their lifetime to the point that they felt very fearful or believed that they or someone close to them would be harmed or killed.
- On a typical day, there are more than 20,000 phone calls placed to domestic violence hotlines nationwide.
- The presence of a gun in a domestic violence situation increases the risk of homicide by 500%.
- Intimate partner violence accounts for 15% of all violent crimes.
- Women between the ages of 18 and 24 are most commonly abused by an intimate partner.
- 19% of domestic violence involves a weapon.
- Only 34% of people who are injured by intimate partners receive medical care for their injuries.

Sexual Assault/Rape:

- 1 in 5 women and 1 in 71 men in the United States have been raped in their lifetime.
- Almost half of female (46.7%) and male (44.9%) victims of rape in the United States were raped by an acquaintance. Of these, 45.4% of female rape victims and 29% of male rape victims were raped by an intimate partner.

Stalking:

- 19.3 million women and 5.1 million men in the United States have been stalked in their lifetime. 60.8% of female stalking victims and 43.5% of male victims reported being stalked by a current or former intimate partner.

Children and Domestic Violence:

- 1 in 15 children are exposed to intimate partner violence each year, and 90% of these children are eyewitnesses to this violence.

Economic Impact:

- Victims of intimate partner violence lose a total of 8 million days of paid work each year.
- The cost of intimate partner violence exceeds $8.3 billion per year.
- Between 21% and 60% of victims of intimate partner violence lose their jobs due to reasons stemming from the abuse.

Source: NCADV.org/statistics

Sexual Assault:

- Every 98 seconds, someone is sexually assaulted.
- 1 in 5 women and 1 in 7 men are sexually assaulted in their lifetime.
- 1 in 8 sexual assault victims knew their attacker.
- 1 in 5 female and 1 in 16 male college students are raped; 90% of the rapes are never reported.
- In FY 2017, the Department of Defense reported 6,769 reports of sexual assault. Note: This figure represents the number of assaults that were reported in 2017, not necessarily the amount that actually occurred in 2017.
- 94% of women who are raped experience symptoms of post-traumatic stress disorder (PTSD) during the two weeks following the rape.
- 30% of women report symptoms of PTSD nine months after the rape.
- 33% of women who are raped contemplate suicide.
- 13% of women who are raped attempt suicide.
- Approximately 70% of rape or sexual assault victims experience moderate to severe distress, a larger percentage than for any other violent crime.
- People who have been sexually assaulted are more likely to use drugs than the general public.
  - 3.4 times more likely to use marijuana
  - 6 times more likely to use cocaine
  - 10 times more likely to use other major drugs

Sexual violence also affects victims' relationships with their family, friends, and coworkers

- 38% of victims of sexual violence experience work or school problems, which can include significant problems with a boss, coworker, or peer.
- 37% of victims of sexual violence experience problems in their relationships with family and friends, including getting into arguments more frequently than before, not feeling able to trust their family/friends, or not feeling as close to them as before the crime.
- 84% of survivors who were victimized by an intimate partner experience professional or emotional issues, including moderate to severe distress, or increased problems at work or school.
- 79% of survivors who were victimized by a family member, close friend, or acquaintance experience professional or emotional issues, including moderate to severe distress, or increased problems at work or school.
- 67% of survivors who were victimized by a stranger experience professional or emotional issues, including moderate to severe distress, or increased problems at work or school.

Men:

- At least 1 in 6 men have been sexually abused or assaulted.
- 16% of males are sexually abused by the age of eighteen.
- Research on male childhood sexual abuse concluded that the problems is "common, under-reported, under-recognized, and under-treated."

Why these statistics are likely underestimated:

- Males who have such experiences are less likely to disclose them than are females.
- Only 16% of men with histories of serious sexual abuse documented by social service agencies considered themselves to have been sexually abused, compared to 64% of women with documented histories in the same study.

Source 1in6.org

Child Sexual Abuse:

- 1 in 4 girls are sexually abused before the age of eighteen.
- 1 in 6 boys are sexually abused before the age of eighteen.
- 1 in 5 children are solicited sexually while on the internet.
- An estimated 39 million survivors of childhood sexual abuse exist in America today.
- 30–40% of victims are abused by a family member.

- Children fabricate their stories of sexual abuse only 1/2% (0.5 percent) of the time.
- 90% of victims of sexual abuse are assaulted by someone they know.

Source: Comfort In The Storm

Sexual Harassment:

- 1 in 3 women and 1 in 10 men are sexually harassed in the workplace.
- 94% of sexual harassment are never reported.
- 90% of individuals in the LGBTQ+ community have been sexually harassed.

Sex Trafficking:

- From 2007 to 2017, the National Human Trafficking Hotline, operated by Polaris, received reports of over 34,700 sex trafficking cases within the United States.
- 1 in 7 endangered runaways reported are likely sex trafficking victims.
- The International Labor Organization estimates that there are 4.8 million people trapped in forced sexual exploitation globally.
- The average age for males and females who are forced to enter the sex trade in the United States is twelve to fourteen years old.
- Between 14,500 and 17,500 people are trafficked in the United States each year.

Effects Of The Hush Topics

Research shows that the effects of the HUSH Topics can be physical, emotional, or psychological. This list includes some of the side effects that a person may have after experiencing sexual violence. A person may experience none or all of the below. If you or someone you know is experiencing the negative effects of their trauma, we recommend that you or they speak to a doctor, therapist, or victim advocate. Remember that these effects are not easy to cope with, but they can be managed with the right help and support system.

Depression

Flashbacks

Anxiety

PTSD

Self-harm

Sexually Transmitted Infections

Substance abuse (alcohol, prescription pills, tobacco, street drugs)

Pregnancy

Miscarriage/Stillbirth

Eating disorders

Sleep disorders

Suicide

Dissociation

Difficulty in establishing relationships

Abdominal pains

Chronic pain

Hypertension

Nightmares

Source: Raiin.org/ NCADV.org/statistics

False Reports

One of the most common questions that individuals ask us during training is "What about false reports?" Some of you may be wondering the same, so let's tackle the question before you read the stories of the survivors, who have courageously decided to HUSH No More.

According to the Department of Justice, only 1-3% of all trauma reports are false. This is due to many reasons, but the most common reason is that some people will lie to hurt others or protect themselves.

When thinking about false reports, consider the following: When a victim files a sexual assault, child abuse, or domestic violence report, this is a major decision. Oftentimes, they have to talk to an investigator who would ask them a lot of questions and at times, take pictures. Depending on the injuries, the victim may have to take a sexual assault forensic exam. If they decide to file charges, they will have to go in a courtroom and testify before strangers about the abuse they endured without being guaranteed that the offender will go to jail.

Oftentimes, family, friends, and co-workers don't believe the victim and will say mean things to them. This will most likely happen if the offender is also a family member or a close friend.

If you raped or abused someone, would you admit to doing the crime? So why would you believe an offender who tells you that they didn't do it?

Today, if I asked you the following questions, how would you feel? Would you respond?

- When was the last time you had sex?
- Was it consensual?
- Did you have an orgasm?
- Did you ejaculate?
- Did you have anal sex?
- Was there any bleeding?
- Do you remember the size of the penis?
- Do you remember any identification marks on the vagina?

Most of you will have a tough time answering these questions to a friend and wouldn't dare tell it to a stranger. These are just some of the many personal questions a victim is asked when reporting their abuse to the police.

Remember that it is NOT EASY to report abuse. Also, remember that you were not at the scene of the crime, so you don't know what happened.

Our Right to Tell It

Society, gossip, and family pressures have created a hostile environment where victims feel as if they must hide their trauma. This leads to feelings of shame, low self-esteem and self-worth, drug abuse, alcoholism, additional trauma, etc. Contrary to the detrimental beliefs of others, victims have a right to share exactly what happened to them and be heard. They have a right to speak or write about their trauma and their abuser. When individuals come forward and share their story, they start to heal and unleash the shame they have been experiencing. Some people may not believe their story or support them after they come forward. Regardless, it's their choice to decide when, how, and if they will ever share their story. The courageous authors in this book have decided that this is the right time for them to share their survival journey with the world to heal and to promote awareness and prevention of the HUSH Topics.

The stories you are about to read are all written and formatted by the authors, and this is their way of coming forward to HUSH No More. They are raw and heartfelt, and they may trigger an emotional response. If this occurs, take time to journal your thoughts and contact a professional to discuss your emotions.

Domestic Violence

BUT I LOVE YOU.

These were the words I heard time and time again. Of course, he had all the reasons to try to explain his actions. I never quite understood how someone who claimed to love me so much was the same person who caused me so much pain. The crazy part is that I knew this was not a smart choice from the beginning. However, I chose to ignore all the signs. Even before we said, "I do," I remember the day we were attending a wedding reception together. Just because a man decided to stare at me, I had to endure the tight squeezing of my arm while at the event. Then, after the reception at his house, I faced intense screaming and more arm squeezing which quickly escalated to pulling, tugging, and slapping. Days later, I was afraid and confused, and the "BUT I LOVE YOU" excuses began and were laid on thick. No, I didn't understand it. No, I didn't think it would happen again. After all, everyone has always said that I had a smart mouth and I made people want to slap me. Frankly, I was just a teen mom looking to right my wrongs. I couldn't fathom walking out on the re-established relationship with the father of my child. Besides, he did apologize.

I never knew love could be used as a weapon, one that was so deadly it almost led me to my death. Just like yesterday, it's so vivid in my mind: the moment I tried to leave, and he decided to place a gun to the side of my head. Sitting on our beautiful white couch, all I could do was cry and pray as our young son stood watching his father threaten his mother with this cold silver gun placed on my temple. I remember asking God to spare my life and please don't let my son see this happen. To think, even after that, he still had the audacity to come back with the same lame phrase, "BUT I LOVE YOU." Hearing his sorry excuse was very different for me this time. This time, I knew I had to escape this madness one way or another. However, I had to be strategic. Albeit very afraid-afraid to leave, afraid to stay, afraid for my son, afraid if I wouldn't be able to make it on my own, just afraid. I had to trust that my life was spared for a reason.

No longer did I allow his antics, his painful insults, his brutal hands, or his "BUT I LOVE YOU" mind games to hold me captive. I found learning to love me was far more valuable than the "love" he could ever provide. Thankfully, I was finally able to get to a space where I could look at the woman who faced me in the mirror and say, "BUT I LOVE YOU."

I had to act on faith and surround myself with people who wanted to see me be better and develop a positive mind-set. I became focused and adamant about creating a better environment for me and my child.

I am still a work in progress. I navigate through life only one step at a time. I continuously talk to myself in the mirror for motivation, strength, and to affirm who I am to me! "BUT I LOVE YOU" is now one of the statements that empower me to continue to love who I am and understand who I am not!

I have shared one of my most personal stories to help you rise in confidence without settling for someone who devalues you. I am also sharing one of the activities that I use with other Survivors.

The Noble Life Activity Moment:

Look at yourself in the mirror and say it out loud while looking yourself in the eye.

BUT I LOVE YOU!

I love You because you are valuable.

I love You and you are worth a healthy relationship.

I love You and you don't have to settle.

I love You because you deserve to be loved.

I love You because you are uniquely you.

Tammy Nobles

Tammy Nobles is the passionate founder and CEO of Tammy R. Nobles - Noble Necessities, LLC, a premier empowerment and development company. For over twelve years, she has inspired and helped others live life intentionally through her ministry, success coaching, and leadership workshops. Tammy is a licensed Minister, and she believes in the power of positivity. She consistently inspires the world through her quotes tagged as #makeitaNOBLEday, her broadcasts known as T.E.A. with Tammy, and her Winning (WINS) day declarations. She is also the author of the *Noble Life Activity Journal*, which provides strategies to help you engineer the life you desire to live. Her favorite quote comes from the Bible: "I can do ALL things through Christ who strengthens me." Philippians 4:13.

Connect with Tammy R. Nobles via her website at TammyRNobles.com. Follow her on Facebook, Instagram, and Twitter. You may also email her at tammy@tammynobles.com.

My Father, My Hero

I can remember my father living at home with us when I was a young girl as part of one large nuclear family. I felt blessed to be living with both of my parents, especially my dad. I was definitely a daddy's girl who loved her father very much. Every day, when I came home from school, I would run into the house to see if he had come home from work. In his free time, he took me fishing with him, told me how beautiful I was, and never made me feel bad. Of all the things he did and said to me, I loved these precious times the most. In my eyes, my dad was the bravest and best man in the world.

I have fourteen sisters and brothers but, in my mind, I was still special in his eyes. I can remember when we all lived in a three-bedroom house. As the years passed, most of my older siblings moved. However, due to a large number of children, many of us still lived at home and had to share rooms.

Up until one particular day, our lives were that of a typical large family. On that life-changing day, late at night, I heard my mom crying and yelling. She was yelling so loud that I awoke suddenly and wondered what was happening. I soon realized that my mother and father were in the middle of an intense fight. I can't recall my parents ever arguing or having an altercation before that day. After that night, I realized that my dad loved to drink, and when he did, many times, his behavior would change dramatically. Change he did that, and for the worse. Dad would often drink and play pool with his friends to relax after work. However, when dad returned home from drinking with his buddies and playing pool, his behavior was oftentimes violent towards my mother. He would chase my mom around the house with a gun, threatening to shoot her and sometimes actually shoot at her. Mom would run across the street to our neighbor's or friend's house for safety. The neighbor or friend would provide safety and shelter to my mom. She would later come back to the house after dad had calmed down or fell asleep.

Although my father was drinking heavily, he still was my hero who I deeply loved, but I started seeing my dad differently. Yes, I loved my father, and as always, he continued to make me feel special; however, my love for my dad clouded my best judgment. I overlooked the violent behavior he exhibited towards my mother. I solely focused on how he treated me and not his violent behavior. Another reason why I overlooked my father's violent acts was because my mother treated me differently from my siblings. Mom never told me how much she loved me or even that she loved me when I was a child. Because I felt as though my mother treated my siblings better than me, I never talked to them about my feelings or the violent behavior I witnessed. In hindsight, I now know that I did not trust my siblings enough to talk about my feelings because I never felt special to them or in my mother's eyes. So, I kept all of my hurt, misgiving, and pain to myself, all wrapped and bundled in my heart.

As I grew up and witnessed how my father treated my mom, I would say to myself, "I will never be with a man who drinks alcohol." No, I didn't want a man who let alcohol turn him into a mean person who hurt the people who loved him the most. I did not want to repeat or accept that kind of behavior in my life. I often think about how dad hurt my mother, but of course, I never blamed dad for his actions. I blamed everything on alcohol and the men with whom he played pool. It had to be their fault; my loving hero would never hurt anyone. Still, no matter what I felt or thought about dad in my heart, the reality was that he would come home drunk, angry, and ready to fight. Many times, the police had to be called. At times, the police would take dad to jail and other times they just talked to him. When dad did go to jail, he would stay in there for a few days to calm down and then be released to return to his old ways. While dad was incarcerated for those couple of days, he would plant a vegetable garden. I remember visiting dad in jail, and he would be so excited to show me where he planted his vegetable garden. I thought, "Wow! This is the most beautiful garden I've ever seen." Though he was incarcerated, I was so proud of him during those times. I guess the incarceration was more therapeutic to him than punitive.

As I said, my dad was a violent man when he consumed alcohol. When my dad remained at home and did not socialize with his friends, he was the best: a kind, loving, and great guy to be around. In those moments, anyone would be proud to call him son, husband, father, or friend. Simply put, he was a good and loving man to all, when sober.

Later in life, our family moved to a different location. Eventually, my mother became a single mother as my dad moved out, and I became a fatherless daughter. As any daddy's girl would do, I cried and cried. I wanted my dad to reside in our family home. I so wanted that and prayed a million prayers for that to be the case. No matter how much I cried and prayed, dad no longer lived with us and it was vastly different: no more fishing trips and no one to say, "I love you." After a while, I began to accept the new normal that dad no longer lived with us. Still, deep in my heart, I could not fathom why I was hurting inside and felt so lost. After all, dad only moved down the street and I saw him every day. But the pain was still there. Although I could see his home from the porch of ours, that wasn't good enough for me. I wanted him home with us. I prayed daily, constantly and fervently, for help to understand why I hurt so much. My grandmother taught me how to pray, so I was determined to pray the hurt away. And yes, prayer became my source of strength. I would pray at night and during many other times, but my pain and hurt never truly subsided or went away. I learned how to mask the pain, and I would pretend that everything was alright. Thinking about my father's beautiful words to me that I was the "most beautiful little girl" kept me going and helped me through many painful times. Every school day, I eagerly looked forward to my dad walking over to see me before I walked to the bus stop.

I was getting used to this new normal, but then that fateful day happened. My dad died. When I found out, I wanted to cry. I tried to cry but the tears would not flow. I remember how my grandmother would say, "When someone dies, you will see that person again." Those words resonated with me as an adult because it was then when I realized how much I really needed my dad. I miss him every day and not a day goes by that I don't think about him. I did not attend my father's funeral, but I can recall watching everyone come back to the house. To this day, I do not know why I did not attend my father's funeral so I could properly say goodbye or get some sense of closure. I would often say that my father is not dead; after all, I did not see him in the casket or see him get buried. I just accepted what was told to me-my father was dead. So, in my mind, for a long time, I would tell myself he was not dead and that I was going to see him again. I kept saying this for a long time, but he never came back.

The decisions that I made in my life and what I witnessed as a young girl affected my life as an adult. I never wanted a man who drank alcohol or smoked because of how those things shaped and impacted my own dad's life. As I grew older, I realized that my dad was an alcoholic and that he had a hard time controlling his temper when drunk. That is why I tried so hard not to date or have relationships with men who drank alcohol.

When I married my now ex-husband, I looked at him as being better than my father while still loving me as much as my father did. However, this matrimony union is when my life really changed, and I became the person I never wanted to be. I was once again living in a house with an abusive man who was an alcoholic just like my dad. However, God is always in control and has a plan for everything. I had to go through witnessing abuse, learning what abuse is, becoming a fatherless daughter, and being in an abusive marriage to get where God wanted me to be-a person who now knows her worth and value. I will no longer HUSH No More but encourage other teen mothers and fatherless daughters by helping them see their worth and value.

Evangelist Geneva Dunn

Evangelist Geneva Dunn is the Executive Director of Butterfly Dreamers, a nonprofit organization helping women who are fatherless daughters and teenage mothers. She is a sought-out speaker when it comes to working with youth and adults of all ages. As a young girl, she gave her life to Christ at the Church of God of Prophecy, in Sanford, Florida, where she began to minister and teach the Word of God to adults, youth, and children. Through the Music Ministry, she also led Mime and Youth Praise Dance Teams. As God moved her to Sweet Heaven Church of God, she became a Minister under Pastor Bobby Butler, where she worked as a Pastor Assistant, Single Ministry Leader, and participated with the Mime and Dance Ministry. Now, Evangelist Dunn attends Agape Worship Center International, under Bishop Vincent Collins. Since being there, she has become an Ordained Minister, licensed by the Church of God, in Cleveland, Tennessee. Evangelist Dunn teaches the Word of God and works with the Youth Ministry, Singles Ministry, and Woman's Ministries, as well as the Music Ministry. Her passions include mentoring mothers in substance recovery, children in mental health facilities, teenage mothers, and empowering youth in the areas of Teenage Dating, Intimate Partner Violence, Self-esteem, and Fatherless Daughters. Evangelist Dunn has three daughters, ten grandchildren, and five great-grandchildren.

The Color of Love

I just wanted to be loved, but doesn't everyone?

Did I settle, just because I wanted a man?

I got a ring, so I thought I won.

The ring is on my eye, but you don't understand.

You are telling me this, but I'm feeling like that.

What do you know about love? He loves me.

You are telling me I got to move one, but he's frat.

But with him is where I want to be.

I want to leave; I really do!

I'm not as strong as you. I'm not you!

I am strong too.

My love is red, not black and blue.

LeDesma Terry

Get Mad

There I stood on the "Red Carpet."

I never dreamed that I would be in so much trouble that I'd have to see the Brigade Commander. The "Red Carpet" was a piece of carpet in front of the Brigade Commander's desk, that soldiers stood on to receive their punishment.

There I stood, scared to death. The Brigade Commander didn't even look up from his computer when he told me, "You are here because your behavior in family housing is unacceptable." I just stood there frozen in disbelief, thinking, "Really?"

Still, without looking at me, he told me "If this behavior continues, you will be removed from on-post family housing, do you understand?"

Without even thinking, I burst into tears and cried out, "Do you want to find me dead?" I fell to the floor sobbing.

"I don't know what else to do. I didn't know who else to call."

I cried a few more tears while still sitting on the floor. Suddenly, I heard my Brigade Commander sternly yell, "Get up!"

I quickly stood up so that we were facing each other. He looked me directly in my face and asked, "Are you done?".

I stood at the position of attention, with boogers and tears running down my face and replied, "Yes, Sir! I'm done."

At this point, I realized I was done with all of it. I was done with my marriage, the Army, and my life.

I felt like I had nowhere to go, and no one who cared.

That night, while sitting in my car, in front of my government quarters, I said to myself, "Forget your stinking quarters, I'm done with all of this." I slowly put a gun to my head and I just cried and cried and cried.

My tears ended when I saw the blue lights; it was the military police. The same ones who previously came when I needed assistance with my husband. They knew me, my car, quarters, and may have thought that I was a joke or another weak female.

The lights turned off. I didn't know what to think or do. I quickly made the decision to put the gun down and jumped out of the car.

The officer exited his vehicle.

"Sergeant!" He called out to me, "Are you okay?"

"Yes! I'm fine," I replied.

"Good, because I don't have time for weak links."

I dropped my hip and folded my arms.

He stepped up to me and whispered, "Don't be a freakin' weak link."

Then he turned around and got back into his car. I don't know if he saw my gun up to my head or not, but he didn't seem to care.

I was heated! I was determined not to be a weak link! This Military Police Officer motivated me to change my life.

The next day, I came up with a solid plan. I filed for divorce, had the locks changed, and shortly after, I moved to my next duty station. There I met and married the soldier of my dreams.

Sometimes, we have to get mad, so we can get right and stop the violence!

LeDesma "Desi" Terry

LeDesma "Desi" Terry is a native of Chicago, Illinois. She is married with two children and currently resides in Elgin, South Carolina. Throughout the years, she has been active as a health and beauty independent consultant for Mary Kay, the Body Shop, and Beauticontrol.

As a retired Army Officer, LeDesma has served in the human service, food service, and logistical fields. She has a host of assignments to put under her belt, including "Operations Iraq Freedom", 2nd Infantry Division, South Korean, 101st Air Assault, and 3rd Infantry Division Rock of the Marne. Her education includes a Master of Arts, Liberty University; Bachelor of Science, Northern Michigan University; Southeastern Esthetics Institute: Licensed, The Nail School of Manicuring, Southeastern Institute; and Licensed Body Work and Massage Therapist. Her favorite quote is, "My gift is worth nothing if it's not given."

Which Domestic Violence story impacted you the most?

_____

What did you learn about Domestic Violence?

_____

_____

_____

List any additional thoughts you may have.

_____

_____

_____

_____

Sexual Assault

I Trusted You Intro

The man I thought I loved turned out to be my rapist. He groomed, manipulated, and played mind games to convince me he was everything he wasn't. Little did I know, he was out on bond for doing this same thing to someone else.

Chapter One: Events Leading Up

On February 9, 2017, someone named Tyreek added me on Facebook. I didn't have any feelings about it because I didn't know who he was exactly; I was just curious. I didn't accept his request right then; I waited a couple of days and then I accepted it. After I accepted his request, he sent me a message on Facebook Messenger, saying I should talk to him and began telling me how beautiful I was and how he was glad he found my Facebook page. He also stated that he thanked God he found my page. He continued to tell me how special I was. I was flattered and felt special; it made me feel like someone might actually care about me and think I'm pretty.

I've always been self-conscious about my weight and my appearance, but I felt like he looked past that. He kept saying that he wanted to come see me and wanted me to go see him, but I didn't really want to because I didn't know who he was. I then started asking people about him to find out more information and who he was exactly. People had different opinions but ultimately, I wanted to find out for myself. After all, his attention made me feel flattered. Eventually, on my spring break of sophomore year, my parents went to take pictures, so I went to go see him while they were out. He was begging me to come see him. My cousin and her friend (who is Tyreek's cousin) were at his grandma's house. This was next to Tyreek's mom's house and they saw me over there. Tyreek and I were just sitting in the car and we kissed and that was about it that day. At that moment, I felt flattered and special, but now I regret even going over there.

A couple of days went by, and I asked my brother on Easter if he knew Tyreek. My brother told me that he knew him and that I needed to stop talking to him if I was. But I didn't stop talking to him. I was flattered by his attention and wanted to see what would come of the friendship.

Tyreek and I kept talking and then, one day in May of 2017, I was at the mall, and he messaged me on Facebook and asked me what I was doing. To see if he would get jealous or angry, I told him I was with my boyfriend even though I didn't have a boyfriend, at the time. I did this to see if he was actually serious about being with me. In retrospect, he didn't react, which shows me that he wasn't being serious, and he didn't care. At that time, I was just caught up in the attention that I was receiving. He asked me to come see him that day and I said, "I guess I could." That day, we just kissed again and that was it.

The last time we saw each other was in May. After that, we stopped seeing each other, but we were still talking up until December. In December, I went to see him one night, after my hair appointment. That night, he forced me to give him oral sex. I didn't really want to do it. When it was over, I left right after. I felt disgusted and confused.

That was the last time I saw him up until April. We were texting in between that time and he would say things like "come see me," even though he had a girlfriend. One day he said some words to me; he called me "dumb" and a "fat bitch." I was confused and hurt. After that, I didn't hear back from him because he went to jail. I didn't know that was the reason he wasn't responding at the time. I learned that afterward.

Chapter Two: That Night

He got out of jail, and I didn't really say anything, but he was still trying to get me to come see him. On April 1st, around 7:00 p.m., he texted me (I was with a friend), and he told me to come see him. I was already out, so I said, "Okay, yeah that's fine, I can". I told my friend, "I'm going to go see Tyreek". She said, "Okay." When he texted me, he asked me if I was going to give him head. Then, he texted me, "We going to the track." When he said that, I was like "Okay?". I felt confused, I didn't really know why we were going there, but I said, "I guess so." I trusted him. I never thought anything bad would happen.

I got to Swansea and picked him up. We went to the track, and when we got there, we didn't really say anything. We were just sitting in the car listening to music. What started out as something consensual quickly turned into something forceful.

He laid his seat back and pulled his penis out of his pants and said, "Go ahead." I didn't really like that he told me what to do; I felt used. So, I gave him head, and he ejaculated. While I was doing that, he said, "Are you going to give me some?" And I said, "No, I don't want to." but he said, "Okay, well just keep giving me head." He ejaculated twice, so I thought he was good. I thought I would be fine and wouldn't have to do anything else. We were just sitting in the car and he was like, "Get out the car." So, I was like, "Why do I need to get out of the car?" He just said, "Get out." I sat there for five minutes, thinking, "What am I getting out the car for?" He said it again, and I thought maybe he just wanted to hug me.

I eventually got out, and he was like, "Oh you got those tight shorts; I'm fixing to get some tonight." And he laughed. I said, "No, you're not" and I walked over to the passenger side of the car. He was looking at me, and I said, "What did I get out the car for?" He walked to me and started rubbing on me. I said, "No, get off me," and he said, "C'mon." I again said, "No, get off me". I felt annoyed because I didn't want to be touched and I didn't want to have sex. I tried to walk back to the driver's side of the car, but he pushed me up against the car so that I couldn't go anywhere. He started to kiss on my neck, and I tried to push him off, but he wouldn't get off of me. I told him to move, and every time I tried to move, he moved with me. He pulled his pants down and I was like, "What are you doing that for? I told you 'no." Then, he goes to pull my pants down, and as he did so, I started panicking and was like OMG, and he pushed me into the car so I was like, "Get off of me Tyreek! What are you doing? Let me get up!" He said, "Let me put the tip in," and I said, "NO! Get off of me please!" I tried to move, and when I tried, he already put his penis in my vagina a little bit so when I moved, it came out. When I tried to get up, he shoved it up my butt. I felt him on top of me; I could feel his emotions, he was laughing about it. I was disgusted, sad, and angry.

When he did that, I said "STOP!" and tried to push him off of me, but he wasn't going anywhere. I kept begging him to stop but he wouldn't. I was crying. After a while, I didn't have any power to do anything to him and my whole body went numb. He finished and then got off of me. I pulled up my pants and walked over to the driver's side. I was in disbelief, and I felt so dirty and I didn't know what to do.

By the time I got to the driver's side, he was already back in the passenger seat. I told him I wasn't taking him home and he laughed and said, "Yes you are." He forced me to take him home. Luckily, his house was only a minute away, so it wasn't far. I didn't say anything; I was just driving. And then he said, "You stress me out." I didn't know what to say as I was in shock. I said, "How could you say something like that after you just violated me and did something I didn't want to do?" he didn't say anything, just laughed and got out of the car. He said, "Text me when you get home." I was confused.

I called my friend on my way back home and told her, "Tyreek just raped me." Being that it was April 1st, she said, "Don't play with me, this better not be a joke." And I told her it wasn't a joke. Between that night and the next day, I struggled and contemplated on if I should speak up about what happened.

I eventually spoke to my sister and gave a brief statement on what happened that Sunday. She took me to the hospital on Tuesday, April 3, 2018, for a medical exam and so that I could tell law enforcement what exactly happened. A month after the assault, I started attending trauma-focused cognitive behavioral therapy.

Chapter Three: The Aftermath

On May 8, 2018, I found out that Tyreek was arrested for First Degree Kidnapping and First Degree Criminal Sexual Conduct and the following day he had bond court. At court, I read a victim impact statement, which was extremely hard for me to do but I knew it had to be done so that he wouldn't be able to manipulate anyone else again, and so that I could have a voice.

In my statement, I explained how hurt I was and how he made my life a living hell. The judge denied his bond and I felt relieved. I felt relieved because the judge listened to me and thought what I said was significant enough to deny his bond at the magistrate level. What I didn't know was that I was going to receive tons of backlash from his family.

His cousin argued with my sister, stating that Tyreek didn't do what I was saying he did to me. I was very upset. His nephew and niece made multiple Snapchat posts about me. His other cousin even messaged me on Snapchat stating that I was lying. She carried on for days though I never replied. They harassed me and slandered my name for no reason at all.

Though I was strong during that, I did want to break down and be silent about what Tyreek did to me. For the next two months, I was doing fine. I attended a preliminary hearing where the judge stated that there was probable cause and stated that there was enough evidence to go on with my case. That hearing also made me feel confident about my story. In June, I was notified that Tyreek and his lawyer appealed his bond being denied and they wanted to have a bond revocation hearing. I felt scared because I did not understand why Tyreek was trying to get out on bond knowing what he did to me was wrong. August 8, 2018 was the first time I saw Tyreek since the attack. That was the day of the bond revocation hearing. Seeing him in a jumpsuit made me sick to my stomach. I stood there in disbelief. He laughed when he saw me which made me realize that he did not care about what he did to me neither did he care about how I felt. My solicitor presented the evidence and his lawyer stated how Tyreek was such a great person, which was a lie. The judge decided not to make a decision that day. I waited for about two more weeks.

On August 22, 2018, I received a phone call from my victim advocate stating that the judge decided to grant Tyreek bond. I felt defeated and I no longer felt the confidence I had before. I just wanted to stay in my room every day and cry. Every day, I asked myself what did I do so wrong? Was this my fault? I was back at stage one again and I hated myself for it.

Chapter Four: Blooming

The next few months weren't great, but they weren't bad. I continued therapy, where I was supported, and my therapist listened to what I had to say. I didn't know therapy would help me, but it did. Therapy helped me realize that I am able to face this situation and that I am not alone. There were some days where I didn't want to go, but I knew I had to so that I could heal and talk about my story. My therapist made me see that I am loved and supported by many people and that the assault just simply wasn't my fault.

While I was attending therapy, I was able to participate in an eight-week yoga therapy group, where I met one of my closest friends. Yoga reduced my anxiety, which helped me a lot. Even though the group is over, I still use the coping skills I learned there when I'm having a bad day or a flashback of the event.

It has now been one year. Last year, I definitely could not see the light at the end of the tunnel, and I rolled my eyes when my therapist attempted to instill hope in the counseling and healing process. But, I have to admit, she was right. I never would have thought that I would be able to talk about what happened and tell my story without being affected.

I feel strong, confident, and ready for whatever may come when it is my day in court. I understand justice may not be served because sometimes in the courts the outcome is out of our control. However, I know that this was not my fault and I will not let the court outcome define my life because I know the truth and so does he. That is something he will have to live with.

This has been an interesting season in my life, to say the least. Sometimes when you are in a dark place, you think you have been buried. I did for sure. But ironically, it is springtime, and just like the flowers around me, I have realized that instead of being buried, I have been planted, and I am now blooming. It's going to hurt; change often does. But hold on, your bloom is coming.

*The name of my rapist has been changed for general legal reasons and to protect the privacy of the parties involved in this ongoing case.

Andrea' Amaker

Andrea' Amaker was born on July 31, 2001 in Columbia, South Carolina. She attended Lexington County School District Two public schools up until May 30, 2019. She received her high school diploma from Airport High School in West Columbia, South Carolina. While in school, Andrea was an A and B honor roll student and exceeded in all her academics. Andrea now attends college where she is majoring in Sociology with a concentration in Criminal Justice. When Andrea receives her degree, she plans on going to law school to pursue her law degree so that she can one day become an Attorney and fight for the little girls and boys who have endured any sexual violence. Andrea enjoys spending time with her family and friends whom she truly loves. Andrea's favorite scripture is "I can do all things through Christ which strengthens me." Philippians 4:13.

Hush No More

In 2016, I had the opportunity to receive training and volunteer with the Sexual Trauma Service of the Midland, in Columbia, South Carolina. I enjoyed the intensive training because it helped me to reflect deeply on my assault stories. On April 12-13, 2019, I had another opportunity to receive training at the "Hive Summit." The Summit was informative, therapeutic, and remarkable. The speakers shared their own gripping stories of surviving and thriving despite the turmoil in their lives. I went away being more encouraged to share my own personal story of pain, processing, and healing. I realize that life is like a race because this is how God mentions it in the Bible. Therefore, the marathon of life always continues. I am a THRIVER as I share my story of survival from a young age. Both training events required me to do personal reflections of my life.

During 2001, when I was recovering from brain surgery, which included me going through physical therapy. I kept a journal for writing down my memories of the events and my reflections. I focused on journaling each memory of the perpetrators in efforts to forgive the individuals who had violated me. Today, as I reflect on the time, I believe the devil was using those memories to interfere in my recovery from brain surgery. Even during the most challenging times, I didn't believe my Lord Jesus, who died on the cross for my sins would push those memories back into my inner thought without purpose. Today, I thank God for allowing me to journal my thoughts which helped me to write my book, *My Inner Thoughts*. My thoughts were focused on relearning to walk, talk, and take care of my newborn son. My thoughts were not on the negativity of old experiences. I recalled my Holy Spirit helping me to take off the hold my negative thoughts had on me because of the trickery of the evil one.

It's now 2019 and I am embarking on revisiting this area for this book. I must pray vigorously due to the taunts of the devil attempting to discourage me. On the other hand, my God in the name of Jesus my Lord encourages me to press onward. I am excited to be a part of a collaboration in order for my story to help others to grow. Also, I can continue to heal those unknown areas that have shaped me into a strong person. Please read, as I allow you to view a small portion of some of the abuse I have experienced during my lifetime.

First, I am around eight years old. I am with my sister at her buddy's house. I recall the female buddy, calling me into the bathroom. I never told anyone about this abuse. In 1997, I decided to make Jesus Lord of my life. I reflected on the memory and I had to forgive her in my thoughts.

Second, I am eleven years old. I had a neighborhood buddy who told me that her high school brother wanted to speak with me. She took me to his bedroom. We had sex. At that time, I did not say anything but went along with this toxic behavior. Again, I didn't tell anyone. I continued to interact with the female buddy for a short period of time.

Third, I am thirteen years old. I am molested physically by the plumber when he repaired my sister's bathroom toilet. I recall the white, male plumber, calling me into the bathroom to ask me a question. My niece looked on like she knew he was up to something. At that time, the male took his hands and placed them in my pants. I pushed his hands away. Today, I continue to wonder, why didn't I tell someone about this molestation.

My God allowed me to realize that my youthful negative experiences caused me to deal with a lot of toxic relationships. I have struggled with "no" not because I don't have a "no" in my voice, but because the guys usually had a manipulative way of handling me. My childhood life led to additional abuse as an adult.

First, I am nineteen years old. I was introduced to a male, but the relationship did not work out. My ex-boyfriend had a male buddy who wanted me to meet his cousin. I agreed to meet his cousin. We played pool. We had sex. Beforehand, I do recall telling him "no," but, I just went along with the sex. I never saw him again. The date was a set-up.

Second, I am twenty-four years old and living on my own after the death of my mother. I met a guy in his thirties. He had plans for me due to my naivety. Our relationship started on a toxic level. He invited me to his apartment to watch a movie. Afterward, he made sexual advances. I just agreed to be a part of this unhealthy relationship. Eventually, I ended the relationship or what appeared to be a relationship. In 1992, I ended the relationship after becoming so fed up with his disrespectful behavior. I cursed him out for being a nonbeliever. I never looked back on that toxic relationship.

Finally, I am twenty-five years old and another older guy comes along. Again, this guy is in his mid-thirties. The relationship was simple with no strings attached. I was over at his place one night watching a movie and eating dinner. My next memory is waking up in his bed with no clothes. I watched the coverage of Bill Cosby and I wondered if the guy I was with had given me something. Again, my toxic mind still did not register the seriousness of his actions. I stopped calling the guy. I learned from experience that there is a quick way to get rid of a toxic relationship. You can ghost them by face or by phone.

I gave these events and memories to God in the name of Jesus my Lord. Today, it is shocking to me to hear, watch, and read all the stories of violation that is present in our society. I am grateful to be a Christian. I am grateful for being a trained Social Worker. Finally, I am grateful that I can reflect on this time in my life without getting overwhelmed.

Today, I still have to seek understanding in this area in order to make sure no unresolved issues have resurfaced. Thus, I had to read the Word of God about this area. There are many stories of sexual assault in the Bible. Tamar was raped by her half-brother; Joseph was seduced by his boss's wife; and Dinah was violated by Shechem's son. All of these true-life Bible stories, helped me to understand this area on a deep spiritual level. I found it challenging in digging deep to pull up such destructive behaviors. But I have peace that lives inside of me. This peace is my Lord and Savior Jesus Christ who has strengthened me to be a strong and courageous female.

In 2002, I had the opportunity to enroll in a social work "Emotional Abuse" training. In 2006, I took a very informative social work "Post Traumatic Stress Disorder" training. I am amazed by the power of God in the name of my Lord Jesus. My God knew exactly what training I needed to heal that hidden part of myself. I now understand the issues that surfaced in my own marital relationship.

In closing, the MeToo movement is not a phase, but it's a reality. I am proudly a part of a group of women whose voices are no longer willing to remain silent. In my case, my voice is being brought forth through my writing. Thus, the stigma can be broken for this fifty-one -year old, college-educated, dynamic female who has chosen to take a stand in writing. I will speak through my writings and HUSH NO MORE.

Ina Smith

Ina Smith was born and raised in the Capitol Hill area of Washington, DC. In the past, she has worked in various government agencies including the South Carolina Youth Advocacy, Federal Emergency Management Agency, Department of Agriculture, and Department of Justice. Finally, she found herself at the Defense Contract Audit Agency, which was located on the former grounds of Cameron Station. Ina is a self-published author who has had the opportunity of speaking in various venues. She was able to share her near-death experience from brain surgery in her book. She started Reveal Ministry to venture into other writing areas to continue the healing process. Ina earned an Associate of Science degree in General Studies from Northern Virginia Community College, a Bachelor of Arts degree in Health Care Administration from Marymount University and a Masters in Social Administration from Case Western Reserve University. She is a Licensed Masters Social Worker. Ina has had the opportunity to utilize her social work skills in the mental health space, working with adults and adolescence. Currently, she works as a Contract Social Worker with the South Carolina Youth Advocacy Program in Columbia, SC. She is the proud mother of two, Marcus and Maya and is looking forward to growing Reveal Ministry by using her voice and writing skills to share her life stories.

My Temple

I didn't realize how far back inside of me my darkest moments were until I had to willfully recall them. It still hurts, bad. I don't like recalling what inspired me to repurpose my life. I'm different now-less hopeful, less sure, confused, and unfocused-because I lost my core values. Well, they were stolen.

Before I turned eighteen, I was abstinent from premarital sex by choice. God was my father. I chose not to swear. I chose not to dress inappropriately. I chose not to wear makeup or fake nails. I chose not to kiss anyone until three months into my first relationship at sixteen. I was in that relationship, pure, through my eighteenth birthday. My values were stolen after my eighteenth birthday.

See, I am a military brat and my mom had a predator working for her. A lot of people do, I'm sure now. I first met Contreras when he was eyeing me down at a work Christmas party the year before. He wore a sweater and kept his distance, but I swear to you, reader, you could see evil all over his eyes. I felt it like an unfamiliar dark shadow. Others avoided him, but he was extremely attracted to my innocence and potential like a vulture.

Meeting this then twenty-one/twenty-two-year old inspired my first book idea, "Devilish Love." No one will ever read the demented, unfinished story I began as a coping mechanism, so here's what it would've been about. "Devilish Love" begins with an uptight girl named Autumn. She marries Joseph, reminiscent of my first partner, but inspired by the virtues of God. Their innocent love story would be maintained until Joseph dies of natural causes and Autumn decides to be a nun. She visits Joseph's grave and meets Devin, who is very shifty, but she decides to trust him anyway. Do you see where this is going? Devin manipulates Autumn and pulls her away from God and Joseph's memory until she loses all her core values and Devin takes her life in the cemetery they met in. Throughout Autumn's time with Devin, he uses her and uses her as she convinces herself she likes it, chose it, and that it's worth it. I'll give you a moment because that's how my virginity was stolen from me.

Contreras kissed me without permission. I told my boyfriend, and we broke up. I was without my close friends for months. For months I let this man rape me, hoping our relationship would become more meaningful and would make up for my virginity. I didn't feel it was my first time. I just looked down, and my virginity was being stolen on his bed. I was in shock. I coped by acting like I wanted it, but it pains me to my soul to this day to know he used me. We were never officially together. He just took and took for as long as he could. He's the first "X" I have tattooed on my ankle.

I tattooed three "X"s on my leg when I was nineteen because Contreras and two others deeply betrayed my trust and distorted my idea of how much control I have over my body. I used to think of my body as a temple, but it feels destroyed. The second "X" is ironically my first love and it hurts differently, in a way I've yet to find words for.

At twenty, I'm recovering, but definitely far from healed. Recently, I went to a church retreat and the pastor asked God to grant all the young girls their virginity back. I cried because God took my virginity the way he did. As much as I'd love my virginity back, it's now the trauma I want gone. It truly doesn't go away; it just becomes easier to deal with on a daily basis.

Sexual assault is too prevalent. Something big needs to change culturally. My word of advice to help with this problem: If you're being forced into sex and can fight back, get violent. Go crazy, because then and there, the perpetrator deserves it. Do it for all of the rapists who got away. Some people don't get "NO," but they sure can get kicked in the groin as hard as possible.

Shakira Monique Stewart

Shakira Monique Stewart is curious, creative, and determined. She consistently works on several of her unpolished story ideas and writes TV scripts, menu descriptions, speeches, etc. Telling stories is her passion; writing is her skill. She also loves people and making positive changes. Shakira wants everyone to know that she loves her family and wishes them the best.

My Thoughts During the Winter of 2013

I have been beaten down, pushed around, and taunted since I was small. For the longest I can remember, a consistent stream of people have hurt me in some horrid way. I have tried taking a stand but have been hit to the ground. I lived in dark corners for days, months, years seeing how no one even cared. I was becoming cold as the blood rushed down my face. My skin slowly turned from a deep red to night blue. I couldn't breathe, I couldn't see, days were becoming dark for all I could feel was a sharp pain. For my shame, I have been kicked around all day and shoved into walls every time I blink. Every time I try to run away, they always seem to find me. They beat me, kick me, and throw me to the ground. They don't stop till I have turned purple or blue or until I'm so swollen and numb and can't bear to move. When I do have a chance to escape, those are the days that I wish could stay. It gives me the time I can to run and hide away., but I don't want to hide for the rest of my life. I want to be free and for someone to care for me, to be treated with respect and not be the girl who is beat for just being herself. I want the dream of me being free to become a reality.

This poem was written in the winter of 2013. After writing it, I convinced myself that the poem wasn't about me, but just an idea I had. Looking back, it was definitely about me.

Eleanor Parker Smith

Speak Up

It was the middle of January, and I was rushing to get ready for school when out of nowhere, I heard a knock at the front door. I was a bit confused because nobody usually comes to our house that early in the morning. I rushed over to the door and opened it to see a few tall men standing outside the door. They were wearing black vests that had the bold white letters HSI across the front. They asked if they could speak to my dad, so I knocked on Kyle's door and let him know that some people were here to speak to him. I walked back to my room to finish packing my bag. Loud footsteps were all around the house, and I got worried that something bad was happening. I walked out of my room to see the men in the vests going through all of our electronics and collecting them. They went into my room and took my laptop, camera, and phone. I was scared and had no idea what was happening. I was in complete shock. One of the men looked down at me and gave me back my phone but didn't give back Kyle's. The same man asked me if I would like a ride to school, but I declined. Not long after that, my mind got fuzzy, and the next thing I knew Kyle was driving me to school. He told me that he got into some trouble, that he was going to be gone for a while, and that my mother was on her way down. It was a lot to take in in a short time I had before I went to school. That whole day at school was just a constant "What the hell is going on in my life?" When I got home, Kyle was packing a small backpack and started to walk next door. He told me, "Wait for Mom, take care of your brother, and always know that I love you." Those were the last words I remember he said before he disappeared.

The next day was a Friday, so I decided to sleep in and not get my ten-year-old brother, Colton, ready for school. I lay in the dark for most of that day just thinking to myself. Colton was completely confused just as I was, but all I could say was that "Mom is on her way, and she is going to take care of everything." The rest of the night just felt empty. The next day Mom arrived with open arms. It had been a while since we had seen her last. With her being in the military and living in California, it was rare for us to hear from her let alone see her. Colton was all about the hugs and love from her, but I was a bit hesitant. Kyle used to tell me that I don't have to say "I love you" to my mom, that I shouldn't call her, and if she wanted to talk, she would call me first. The hardest one to take was "If she really loved you she wouldn't have left, or she would still be here."

Talking to her again was hard because the way she gave my brother and me affection. I felt this sickness building up inside of me and thought, "Is this real or just show to make us feel better about ourselves like Kyle said?" Mom stayed with us the whole time and never left our side. One day around the end of January, she escorted my brother and me to see a woman about a forensic interview. I didn't exactly know what it was going to be like. They took me into this big room, quite comfortable. The woman started to ask me about Kyle and questioned if he had "done anything" to me. I was uncomfortable and scared to say what happened between us. Sitting nervously in the chair, I didn't say much. I didn't tell her about how he used me to get off, that I was like his own little play toy, that he dressed me up like I was a baby, and I feared if I said anything Kyle would find out and hurt me. I left not saying any of this and just went home and continued my life.

It was a little after February, and Mom had to go back to California to do her military assignment. She found out my Aunt Sherri, Ri, was in Texas, and she was willing to take my brother and me in while Mom was in California. Mom gave Colton and me a big tote and told us, "Whatever you can fit in this goes with you." We ended up leaving a lot behind. All I brought with me were my yearbooks, two weeks' worth of clothes, some word puzzles, journals, and just little toys or stuffed animals I could fit. It was Valentine's Day when we headed up to Dallas, and the drive was long and boring-four hours is a long time for us teens. Mom dropped us off with Ri and her kids and left the next day. It was hard to see her leave again, and the living condition wasn't all that great being where we had to sleep on air mattresses and had to share two closets between me, Colton, our cousins (Jade and Lee), Grandpa Dale, and Aunt Ri. It was hard, but it got easier.

One day. we were making pizzas and we're going to sit and enjoy some anime. I wanted to help Ri with the pizzas, so I began to pull out one, and then everything went south. As we pulled out one of the pizzas, I burnt my hand on the metal rack and flipped the pizza upside down onto the tile floor. I went into panic mode about how I had ruined the pizza, not thinking about my hand at all. I fell over into the corner and started shaking, fearing and beating. Ri rushed over to me to see if I was okay, and I wouldn't stop moving away and crying. Eventually, she got me to calm down, and I knew she knew something was wrong. She sat me down later that night and talked to me about a similar experience she had, like what I had with Kyle. I thought I was the only one that went through such mental and physical abuse. She also told me about how she was sexually abused, and out of nowhere something clicked in my head and said, "This is not right; people cannot get away with abusing others any longer."

A couple of weeks later, I went back down to New Braunfels to go back to see the forensic interviewer for a second interview. I told her all the horrible things Kyle did to me. I did not know how to describe things, so she taught me a new word, grooming, and it was sickening to think back to all the things he did, but I said everything. Leaving that interviewer, I felt this weight lift off my shoulders, and I knew that I did the right thing. Kyle would not get away with what he did any longer.

Now the process after that was not easy because I was constantly moving towns and schools, started attending therapy, and wasn't able to use social media without fear of being watched. In May 2015, a little over a year after I did my second interview, Kyle was arrested. June of next year, he pled guilty and was sentenced to thirty-five years with no parole. I finally felt safe, and the fear of him finding me was over. I have never felt as safe as I did until that day, and it was definitely one of those surreal feelings.

To this day, I honestly believe that if I did not go back for a second forensic interview, Kyle would still be out there. The process of working through what happened between Kyle and me, being in hiding, and now being on my own has been and still is hard, but I'm pushing through. I sought out help from anyone I could, friends, family, therapists, even websites. They have all helped me through my tough times, and I came out stronger. I know it's hard to talk to others about problems, that fear building up inside of you; it was something I didn't want any more. I realized that men and women are getting away with sexual abuse every day. Don't let them. Take your voice back. Stand up and show them you are not afraid anymore. I am not a victim. I am a Survivor. You can be a Survivor, too. Speak up.

Eleanor (Ellie) Parker Smith

Eleanor (Ellie) Parker Smith is a twenty-year old college student studying culinary science. She was born and raised in Texas until she was fourteen. Ellie enjoys traveling and has visited countries like Guatemala, El Salvador, and the U.A.E. She is an avid photographer and sword fighter in a LARP community known as Amtgard. She has been a survivor for over six years and an advocate for helping against sexual assault, as well as an ally of the LGBTQ+ community. She shares her story to raise awareness of child assault and sexual assault, and she encourages victims and survivors to come forward and speak up.

Which story Sexual Assault story impacted you the most?

_____

What did you learn about Sexual Assault?

_____

_____

_____

List any additional thoughts you may have.

_____

_____

_____

_____

_____

Child Sexual Abuse

Freddy Krueger

When I think of the '80s, the first thing that comes to my mind is *Nightmare on Elm Street*, a dark and quiet room, the smell of alcohol, the touch of hands, warm objects, and a wet bed. When I was seven, Freddy Krueger entered into my room, causing my life to freeze into a world of darkness. I was alone in a nine-by-seven dark room when suddenly my door opened. My drunk uncle stumbled into my room and fell on top of me and grabbed my vagina with his warm hands. I tried pushing him off me, but his strength overpowered me. He covered my mouth and said, "Hush, you don't want to wake Mom [my grandma and his mother] because you know she's going to whoop your ass if she gets waken up." He said all of this while grinding on me. My uncle began to play in my vagina with his fingers. I kept asking my uncle to get up, and I continually tried to push him off of me, but his strength was too powerful for me. At this point, all I could do was let the tears run down my face. I knew something was wrong, but I wasn't 100 percent sure what was going on.

After the first night, my uncle became very bold and powerful over me. He continued to come into my room and started using sex toys and having oral sex on me. The first time he used a sex toy, it was very painful. I tried to get up, but my uncle pushed me down and covered my mouth. I finally got free and ran to my grandma, who was sitting in the living room drunk. I was trying to tell her what was happening to me, but she did not want to hear it. She replied, "Stop lying, you little bitch and go back into your room. You are always going to be a little bitch, on your back and have a house full of kids." My uncle was standing behind me with a smile on his face while I was trying to tell my grandma. This made my uncle more powerful. I had no one else to tell who would believe me. I went back to the room with teary eyes and asked God to help me. During this difficult time of my life, I was happy to see Sunday through Friday because Freddy Krueger would disappear until Saturday night. He knew that my family would be drinking and getting high, so they wouldn't pay me any attention. Looking back, I can tell you that my uncle molested me almost every Saturday night, for three and a half years. This didn't stop until God heard my cry and sent me some angels.

My little body was crying out for help, but I was scared to tell anyone because I didn't think they would believe me. The fact that I was silent probably made my uncle more powerful and aggressive. Thankfully,

God placed some awesome teachers and friends in my path that took me under their wings. The angels were my first escapes from Freddy Kruger. I began to stay over at their houses on the weekend. My life started to get better, but I was still in a world of darkness. I was always scared to return home, just to be all alone in my dark room. Since I had started staying over at my teachers' and friends' houses, my uncle had stopped molesting me because I always tried to stay away.

Unfortunately, my uncle found another victim. She was a paralyzed little girl who could hardly speak or move. My grandma was responsible for watching her on the weekends. Whenever I was home, my nightmare continued. I had to lay in my bed quietly and pretend like I was asleep. On these nights, I tried not to breathe to stop the tears from flowing while I watched my uncle do the same thing to this little girl that he had done to me. I was very sad that I couldn't help her because I was scared that my uncle would begin to molest me again. I felt like I couldn't say anything because, like my grandma, no one would believe me.

I watched my uncle molest her numerous times until, one day, things changed. The little girl had contracted a sexually transmitted disease. Everyone was tested and my uncle was the only one that carried the same sexual disease that the little girl had. An investigator came to talk to me and finally, I had the courage to tell him about the little girl, but not what he had done to me. I was scared to talk about me because I was ashamed, embarrassed, and my grandma and family told me not to say anything. The fact that I told what happened to the little girl led to both of us being free from being sexually molested by Freddy Krueger. My uncle was sentenced to fifteen years in prison. Mostly, I was free from my uncle's physical abuse, but the emotional and mental abuse lasted a long time afterward. I continued to live in a world of darkness until my uncle died.

Shortly after his death, God reconnected me on social media with my good friend, Dr. Vanessa Guyton. I soon learned that God had placed on her heart to coin "Hush No More." I watched and listened to her for over a year and decided to stand with her and "Hush No More." For now on, my mouth will speak out to help empower children and to bring awareness to prevent child molestation, sexual assault, and abuse. Despite all I have gone through, I will continue to live in the light and remember that I am a Survivor, and I am Somebody!

Tina Wynette Williams

Tina Wynette Williams was born in a very a rough, low-income community formerly known as The Compound, A.K.A Bokey, officially Sanford, Florida. As a child, she was faced with physical abuse, verbal abuse, child molestation, and being categorized as SLD (Specific Learning Disability). Tina was placed in the foster care system, where she had to quickly grow up and become a mother figure and protector of her younger sister. Her life changed when her sixth grade reading teacher taught her to effectively read and write for the first time. This was the first step to her life blossoming to its full potential. Since that day, Tina overcame the odds and was transferred into advanced classes, graduated from high school, and earned a college degree.

Currently, Tina works for the Seminole County Public School System. Additionally, she mentor and tutor young children to reach their full potential and encourages them to "Let Your Voice Be Heard." She has a beautiful daughter and a handsome son whom she loves dearly. In her free time, she writes theater plays and cooks for her community. Her life motto: I am an example of what God can do. He made something beautiful out of this Survivor. For that reason, I am somebody.

Between Sisters

I'm not saying it didn't happen.

I just don't remember that day.

What do you want me to say?

Yes, I believe you!

Why do I have to say "he hurt me too"?

If you already know the truth.

Please, just let me be!

Yes, his voice and his smell haunt me.

This is my truth, and you have yours.

Pushing him out of my mind helps me feel free.

Choosing not to remember is my sanity.

LeDesma Terry's biography is shared under her Domestic Violence stories.

Finding Purpose In The Pain

Most of us remember important dates like our birthday, our children's birthdays, anniversaries, holidays, and a host of other special occasions. However, for us, April 1, 2008 will always be a date we will never forget. That is the day our fifteen-year-old daughter disclosed to us that she had been sexually abused by her cousin between the ages of eleven and fourteen. We can remember it like it was yesterday.

It was a typical Tuesday evening and we were in the kitchen discussing the day's events and the fact that our daughter's grades continued to plummet. This had seemingly become a running conversation between us as we struggled to understand why our daughter had gone from an A student to a D student in what felt like a very short period of time. Our daughter had been sitting in the other room and she must have overheard us, but we weren't prepared for what was to come next. I don't think any parent would have been ready. Approximately an hour after our conversation in the kitchen, my daughter came into the den where I was sitting and sat next to me on the couch. She appeared to have been crying as she handed me a handwritten letter. I took the letter from her and began to read it.

My heart raced, and my mind became foggy as I read her apology for not telling us sooner that her cousin had sexually abused her over a period of three years. She explained that it always took place at her grandmother's (paternal) house after school. She went on to say that she had concerns about how exposing the abuse would impact her grandmother; she worried what her father might do to her cousin if he found out about the abuse, and she didn't want to be the reason the family broke up. She said she had been carrying the secret of her abuse for years, but after hearing us discuss her grades and her poor attitude, she just couldn't carry it any longer. As I looked up from the paper in pure shock and confusion, I blurted out one of the worst responses - "Is this a joke?" After all, it was April 1st. However, within seconds, I realized it wasn't a joke and we were both in tears. My next response was a screeching shrill, "Richhhhhhh!"

Her father rushed in the room as I am holding her in my arms and all I could do was hand him the letter. I had no words. As he read it, his facial expressions resembled the same shock and confusion I had just experienced. He kept looking up at the both of us as if the words on the page were going to make sense at any moment. He may have spoken a few words, but to be honest, my mind was so foggy at that moment, I can't even remember what, if anything, he might have said. I just remember feeling him pivot towards the door as I sat on the couch and I literally reached back without even looking up and caught his arm. "Where are you going?" I asked, and as if I didn't know the answer. He responded,

"You know where I am going!" As I read through the hurt and rage that reverberated from his whole being, I said, "You know you can't do that." He looked powerless.

Within minutes, we were on the phone with the police. They were on the way. We called the boy's parents and told them what our daughter had just disclosed and unapologetically let them know we were seeking to have him arrested immediately. They understood. The police arrived within the hour; a female officer and a male officer. We explained to them what our daughter had disclosed and the female officer requested to speak with her in private. We complied. They also asked if there were other children in the home, so we told them we had a younger daughter as well. They asked for permission to speak with her too. After they briefly interviewed everyone in the home and confirmed with our daughter that we weren't aware of the abuse; the abuser didn't live in our home, and she didn't feel unsafe in our home, they advised us that the report would be turned over to a detective and we should expect to hear from someone the next day.

Sleep evaded us that evening. We kept asking each other how this could have happened. Why didn't she tell us? And what signs could we have possibly missed? We had prided ourselves on the fact that our children never went to daycare because we wanted to make sure they were safe and protected at all times, and yet the danger was around us all along! Rage, devastation, and confusion still can't adequately describe that sinking, sickening feeling we were experiencing. We had one job…protect our children. We felt like we had failed. The clock ticked and night turned into day.

That morning we gave our daughter the option to stay home from school, but she decided she would rather go. Remember, the revelation of her abuse was only new to us, so she was moving in a way that felt normal to her. On the way to school, I made yet another monumental, albeit well-intentioned, error. I started asking questions about the abuse, and while she answered me, I now know that was the wrong thing to do. She needed to be able to process her trauma in a controlled setting with a trained professional, not in the car with her mother. After I dropped her off at school, I called in to work and let them know I wouldn't be in for a few days. We needed to focus all of our energy on our daughter.

I took a shower and cried. I got dressed and cried. I fell on the floor in agonizing pain and tried to pray, but all I could do was cry. I drove to my mother's house and cried all the way. I drove to the church of a pastor we knew who specialized in Christian counseling, but there was no one at the church, so I cried on the steps. So many thoughts raced through my mind and they were all drenched in tears. How and why did this happen to our child? Why didn't she feel like she could come to us and tell us? More tears fell.

We were contacted by Detective M of the Special Victims Unit at our local police precinct. He explained that his department was trained to handle cases involving sex crimes, including crimes against children. The detective was pleasant and requested to speak with our daughter, so we took her to the station for another interview later that day. He assured us that he would give the case his full attention. And, with the help of my husband and other family members, the abuser was arrested the following evening. After being questioned, he confessed. Of course, however that was only the beginning.

Over the next few days, we had arranged for our daughter to see a doctor so she could be examined, and we began interviewing counselors. We were also contacted by Social Services and they advised us that they would be conducting their own investigation as well. We tried to keep the lines of communication open with our daughter, but without exposing her to too much. However, she didn't appreciate us trying to shield her because she felt like she deserved to know what was going on around her. After all, we had just learned of her abuse, but she had been carrying the burden of the trauma for several years and telling us actually caused a weight to be lifted. At that point, she simply needed to feel a sense of control in her life again.

I received a call from my daughter that Thursday saying Detective M was at her school and she had been summoned out of class. She was embarrassed by the police's presence because while he thought he was being discreet, other students in the office began questioning her about why the cops were there to see her as she entered the office. I immediately called the school, but he had already left. I called his cell phone and asked him why he had shown up to her school unannounced and explained how embarrassed she was. He said as part of the investigation, he needed to speak with the victim away from their parent(s) to ensure they weren't involved in or aware of the abuse. He also needed to be sure the child wasn't being coached about what to say or what not to say. I reassured him that we were more than willing to cooperate and if any additional interviews were needed, I would bring her to the place of his choosing, but he was not to visit her at school anymore. He agreed.

The same day, we also received a call from the social worker assigned to our daughter's case. He said he too had just been to my daughter's school and he wanted the name of the school her sister attended so that he could go and interview her as well. I was furious! I told him that he should have contacted me before showing up at her school because between him and the police, they were causing her undue trauma. She was a fifteen-year-old girl in a whirlwind of people coming at her from all sides and at school no less. How could they even think that made sense or helped to maintain her privacy? I immediately told him he was not to attempt to visit her at school again and I refused to give him the name of my younger daughter's school. I informed him that we called the police to begin with so we had absolutely nothing to hide. I also told him if he needed to meet with our children, he could do it in our home. I just needed a date and time. He scheduled us for Saturday morning, and after I blasted him for how he had approached me, he apologized and said he wasn't aware that we had called the police to file the report. He also commented about how so many parents protect their child's abuser, so he had no way of knowing if we were part of that group. He came that Saturday morning, interviewed the kids, and immediately acknowledged that we hadn't been involved in or aware of the abuse and closed the case.

Over the next several days, we secured a counselor. Our daughter started her sessions and we still grappled with how this could happen right under our noses. We had to face the fact that we missed so many signs. Our daughter went from being easy-going and happy to sullen and angry. We blamed it on hormones. She had even started asking us if she could go home after school instead of going to her grandmother's house, and while there was a time we couldn't pry her away from grandma's house, we again blamed it on being a moody pre-teen/teenager. She began to pick up weight and was layering her clothes even in the summer months. Again, we thought it was just teenage hormones.

She became isolated at school and her friends were changing. We just thought it was kids being kids and trying to figure out the whole middle-school thing. She even body-slammed a player during a co-ed basketball league game, and while it was completely out of character, when she said she didn't like the way he was guarding her we didn't think much more about it. She was becoming mouthy with teachers and, as we mentioned before, her grades dropped dramatically. She would say things like she just couldn't focus, but she couldn't tell us why. Again, we were thinking we were dealing with a hormonal high-school student. Although these signs occurred periodically over several years, we missed them all!

As time went on, we experienced tremendous guilt and shame. We thought we were pretty good parents and yet our daughter had been sexually abused by someone in our own family for several years and we had no idea. He had us completely fooled. He was nice, helpful, and present. He even coached her in basketball after school. He was a textbook example of why 90 percent of kids who are sexually abused know their abuser and why the abuse can go on undetected for extended periods of time. He had the two major components every predator needed: access and opportunity. And, because of his familial status, we never suspected he could be capable of harming our child in the most heinous of ways.

Even after we began to educate ourselves on the grooming patterns of predators and the cycle of abuse, we still felt guilt and shame. However, we never hid the fact that our daughter had been abused. Nor, did we ask her to hide it either. It was always her story to tell to whomever and whenever she wanted. We even started a blog as a family, comfortinthestorm.com, to chronicle the experience because we didn't want other children and other families to endure the trauma of sexual abuse. But even with that, there was still a residue of guilt and shame that remained because we felt we had failed to protect her.

We also realized that there was no one we could talk to about the experience our family was dealing with. Moreover, as a parent, you're already feeling like such a failure, and you never wanted it to seem like you were centering yourself in the situation. And, since people treated it like such a taboo subject, who could you trust to hear your pain and empathize without judgment? Even when we tried to talk to those closest to us, their eyes would swell with tears and you could see their heart ache for our child and for us, but there also seemed to be emptiness behind their gaze because they couldn't imagine what that kind of pain felt like.

There were seemingly no support groups for parents of survivors in our community either, so we navigated the unchartered terrain day by day. Who could we ask about how to deal with the police, the District Attorney, our kids' schools, or Social Services for that matter? How were we supposed to deal with our own issues, individually and as a couple? We did, however, have a few sessions of family counseling. In retrospect, we were just looking for some other parents to tell us that they had been through it and their child was okay, so our child was going to be okay too. Over the years, we met one or two families that could relate, but inevitably, we became that voice for other parents through Comfort In The Storm.

From a Christian perspective, we had very different responses. Her dad still felt very strong in his faith and never doubted or distrusted God. However, the mom in me had a falling out with God. I railed against him with questions like, "Where were you while my daughter was being abused?' "How can I trust you when you let this happen to my daughter?" And, "How can you say you love us, and you let such awful things happen?" I was completely blindsided in my faith, and if I am being honest, I just felt like all of our years of service to Him and the church should have insulated our child from such trauma. It took several years for me to find my way back to God and to see my faith fully restored. Mind you, I was still attending church *every* Sunday. I was simply there because my husband was in the ministry, and I felt like I "was supposed to be there."

In case you are wondering, after months of seeing the worst side of our "justice" system, our daughter's abuser was offered a plea deal. He accepted it and was sentenced to five years in jail. He had spent six months in jail from the time he was initially arrested and the time he was sentenced, so he was out after an additional three and a half years or so. Of course, we have plenty of stories we can tell about the courts and the legal process as well, but we will hold those for another time. Just know, it often felt like the rights of the abuser were of greater importance than the rights of our daughter, the actual victim.

It's been eleven years since that Tuesday evening on April 1, 2008. We have weathered the storm and somehow found purpose in our pain. We will not tell you the journey was easy, because it wasn't. We will, however, tell you that healing is possible. It will look different for every survivor and their family. Some marriages will make it, and some will not. There will be days when you feel like the weight of the knowledge your child was violated in such a heinous manner is going to crush you, but then you have to remember that your child is depending on you not to break. Because, with everything they have had to carry, the last thing they need is to feel responsible for your brokenness. We aren't saying you can't feel or even exhibit a range of emotions in the process, we are simply saying that you can't stay in those spaces because to a certain extent, part of their journey to healing involves knowing you are okay.

We continue to find purpose in our pain through our organization, Comfort In The Storm, LLC. We became certified child advocates, and we conduct child sex abuse prevention and awareness training for parents, caregivers, youth-serving organizations, and anyone who is entrusted with the safety and well-being of children. We also have a social media presence where we provide daily prevention and awareness tips on both Instagram and Facebook @comfortinthestorm. Our mission is to help protect children from the trauma of child sex abuse: one family, one social media post, and one training at a time.

Warning Signs for Parents

Changes in behavior provide possible warning signs that a child is being or has been sexually abused. Keep in mind that if your child exhibits one of these behaviors, it doesn't necessarily mean that your child is or has been abused. However, if they are exhibiting multiple signs or behaving in a manner that is inappropriate or causing you concern, we encourage you to talk to your child and seek professional help, if necessary.

- Behavior changes and outbursts
- Mood changes – withdrawn, depressed, angry, or anxious
- Attitudinal changes towards specific people
- No appetite
- An excessive layering of clothing especially in warm weather
- Bed wetting
- Acting out sexually and/or have an inappropriate level of knowledge about sex for their age
- Promiscuity
- Nightmares
- Genital issues – tearing, bleeding, odor, swelling, or STIs
- Running away (prevalent with older kids)
- Pregnancy
- Alcohol and substance abuse
- Fearing or avoiding affection

Disclaimer: Comfort In The Storm, LLC does not provide legal advice or therapeutic services.

Richard and Kathy Butler

Richard and Kathy Butler are Child Advocates and the Founders of Comfort in The Storm, LLC, an organization created to provide education and awareness about child sexual abuse and prevention. Together they are on a mission to end child sex abuse, one speaking engagement, one social media post, one organization, and one family at a time. Kathy holds a Bachelor of Science degree in Communications and received her certificate of completion in Child Advocacy Studies Training from Athens State University. She is also a Court Appointed Special Advocate for Fulton County CASA. Richard served in the U.S. Army National Guard for seventeen years where he was responsible for overseeing communications and readiness training for over twenty-five hundred soldiers. He received his Associate of Arts Degree from Columbia College and has held his ministerial license for over fifteen years. Additionally, Richard serves as a Cadre Facilitator and Court Appointed Special Advocate for Fulton County CASA. The Butlers also recently became Community Ambassadors and they are creating a nonprofit to bring awareness and prevention to the epidemic of child sexual abuse.

Molestation and Manipulation

How do you protect an innocent individual from horrific childhood sexual molestation? No one knows the answer. There are no answers; there are only practices, focused attention, and communication. Being aware of your child's motives, actions, and desires gives parents more of a chance to protect their child from sexual abuse. As I sit down to write this story, my only hope is that parents will take this short story and apply it to their parenthood lives. There is no mistake here; everything that was done to me, was a lack of responsibility by the parents.

I was with my All-American football player cousin. I wanted to be so much like him! He was loved and cheered by everyone in the family. I would ask my grandmother and my cousin's mom if I could stay over for the weekend just to feel "part of" or to be "cool." "Yes, you can stay over, listen and follow all directions that are given to you," my grandmother told me. Once we got to their house and the day passed, it was time to shower and go to bed. "You both get in the shower together and clean up," his mother said. That was the most memorable shower I've taken. My cousin began to lather me with soap and then began to fondle me, asking me if I had ever done anything with a guy. My answer was no. I was only seven years old; he was a few years older than I. I only wanted to be cool and be accepted. He began to rub on my buttock and kiss me. I was not aroused by the sexual acts, but I sensed this would make me closer to him and accepted by my peers. I assumed that this is what cool people do when they spend the night over. I gave into his provocative peer pressure. He took advantage of me in all the ways he could, even things that I don't do as an adult now. Once he finished penetrating me, he said, "Don't tell anyone, you know no one would believe you, and I could get in so much trouble if they found out this happened." He also said, "I'm your best cousin," and that I will always be his. It happened several more times. This time, anywhere we could be alone. From his grandmother's house to my grandmother's, all the way until his family moved away from Sanford. As weeks and months passed by, I lost the feeling of being special to someone. I lost my favorite cousin, not knowing that what he had done to me was just another example of being taken advantage of.

While reminiscing and not understanding what had happened to me, a desire to have another encounter built stronger and stronger. At this time, I was about nine years old, and I would go down the street to play with the other children of my age. I walked into one of my friends' homes to get something to drink and I saw my friend's father sleeping on the couch. Curiosity struck me. He was laying down on his back, and his pants were bulging out. All I could think of was another sexual encounter with a guy. I walked up to him and grabbed his crotch. He laid there, unbothered, still asleep, I thought. I went to grab his crotch again, and he moved around, without opening his eyes, yawning. I interrupted his yawn to ask if I could get something to eat. He said yes, and the day continued as usual. As I was leaving from where he was laying, I felt exalted, sneaky, overexcited, somewhat completed, and my sexual curiosity was fulfilled. I consulted with myself that this was not right. At the time, I had no idea that my actions were a direct result of the sexual abuse done to me by my cousin. Regardless, this was another failure by a parent, because he should have stopped me and corrected the sexual behavior of a nine-year old boy.

Late that night, I went back down the street to my neighbor house to "hang out." I knew that he would be wearing some balling shorts that showed his crotch print. But I had no idea that I just opened a door that would lead me to more mental and sexual despair. I went to the back screen door, and before knocking, the father got up to unlock the door. This time I didn't ask for my friend, nor did the father mention him. The conversation was basic: How was your day? What did you learn in school? Then, he continued to smoke his cigarette and he asked me to come out with him, and walked into the backyard, behind his van. He pulled out his penis and began to urinate. He asked for me to pull out mine too. As he finished peeing, he flicked his cigarette and grabbed my penis and began to stroke it. He pulled me closer and asked if I have started choking my chicken. I had no idea what he meant. I said, "no." He said, "Let's get in the van, and I'll show you." We went into the back of his van that was very spacious and roomy. He started to stroke my penis, and he grabbed my hand and put it on his crotch and said, "Choke my chicken." We masturbated for at least an hour. I didn't ejaculate. But he did, and when he did, he forced me to my knees and sprayed my face. I was speechless and unaware of what had just happened. But he embraced me with a hug, and he said, "You are my boy, don't tell anyone. This is our secret."

Again, I was trapped by someone else's words. His words fulfilled every emotional need I had. I felt a sense of belonging, a sense of love, territorial. Then it happened again and again, until a year later when I ejaculated. My first climax with a forty-five-year old man provided every mental and emotional need I could think of. As I grew older, we became more attached, more adventurous, risky, spontaneous, and planned events. I would lie and say I was going to church with his family, knowing that only his wife and son would be gone to church. During this time, I would be at their home the entire time, performing sexual acts. Once I got older and started to need things for school, I began to seek him out financially. Then it was sexual favors for money, and for my emotional needs. At the age of twelve, I thought that he was the only one that loved me.

The reason I thought he was the only one that loved me was because of my home environment. I was taken from my mother because of child neglect and went to live with my paternal grandmother. My new home was full of discord, betrayal, hate, confusion, jealousy, drunks, mental and verbal abuse, envy, and a lifetime of unforgiveness. I was placed in a home with a sixty-five-year-old lady that was a single mother, who had raised seventeen children of her own. She didn't know love, and for that same reason, she couldn't give love. Not the love that requires a parent to be mindful of their children 24/7. Essentially, she was unable to provide that motherly protection. I was poor, mentally and physically abused, and ridiculed in my father's absence, as he was serving a twenty-three-year prison term.

The neighbors I was allowed to visit, was a middle-class family, with one son, and they had good jobs. My friend was a year younger than me, and he had everything a child would ask for, and his parents encouraged him to share with the neighborhood children. I am sure that I was not supposed to share his father.

Unfortunately, these events happened, and they continued to happen until I was seventeen years old. I heard a few times in church that homosexuality was wrong. This when the spiritual battle of the mind, started fighting against a sexual hungry pedophile, giving me everything that I was not getting from home. Speaking of home, my household got worse. The physical abuse became more frequent, the nights were longer, and pain lingered for days. The mental abuse got worse, on the day that I walked to the front door of my house at the age of fourteen. I overheard my two uncles, an aunt, and several neighborhood friends of my uncles all outside on the porch saying, "You know he down there getting fucked? His faggot ass." "Yeah, I know he be down there late at night, the only thing they could be doing is fucking." "No, are you serious?" another voice said. "Hell yeah, you know that man was fucking them other boys? You know they say he is gay." "Well, your nephew is down there too." "Shit, I don't care, he isn't my son" After hearing this, I grew a sense of hate and rebellion. I hated what I heard and focused my attention on my neighbor that I thought loved me, although he was sexually assaulting me.

Once, I became eighteen, I left home, knowing that what I had been through would only hunt me. As I grew older, I was hurt, confused, unworthy, lost, and unsettled with what was going on in my life. So, I searched for love in all the wrong places. A few years later, I had to revisit my past to understand the trauma I had experienced and the sum of my actions, but rather the actions of people that were well aware of what they were doing to me. I couldn't understand why none of the adults that were in my life, did not stop what was happening to me.

I went to a counselor and she helped me connect the dots. She helped me to understand that what had happened to me was the will of someone else, and all I was looking for was someone to love me. I struggled, not knowing what love was, how to show love, and how to recognize love when it was presented to me. I hated myself for so many reasons that had nothing to do with me. As the counselor concluded her sessions, she would ask, "Is love your mission or your desire?" I answered, "Who doesn't want to be loved?", She replied, "Who wants to be loved?" I said, "Me." Then she would ask, is that a mission or a desire? "I guess a desire." I said. She responded, "You are correct. It's a desire, and something that no one should take advantage of. You were not loved, and that's why you searched for it so much, because you gave it so much. Never allow your want for love to overcome your purpose to give love." As I walked out the door, she would say, "Love and be loved." She helped me to understand so much because from her I learned:

It's nothing wrong with a want or a desire for love, but don't put yourself in a bad situation because you want love.

Love is grown from the seed GROUND=FOUNDATION and a tree needs

WATER= FAMILY
SUN= SELF-LOVE

To be a better tree, it embraces its environment and branches off to spread love.

My Advice to Parents

Parents, I feel obligated to share with you my personal advice, that includes four actions that you can take to prevent your child from being molested.

1. Communicate. I am a father of twin girls, and I communicate with them as much as I can about being open with me. My first conversation with my girls was extreme for the age of seven, because I did not hold back. For this reason, I feel confident that if anyone approaches them sexually, they will be knowledgeable and feel comfortable to tell me. I express to my girls all the time, no matter what happens, tell me. No matter who it is, where it is, tell me. Having an open line of communication with your child is the best defense you will have against what society exposes to him or her. I know, it's hard and sometimes it's out of our control. However, we can empower our children with knowledge, boldness, and courage.

Being raised in an African American family, we were not taught to communicate. Instead, we were taught to shut up, hush, and be quiet. For example, I have a very close cousin, who told me that she told her mom that her uncle was making sexual comments towards her. Her mother made three mistakes. She didn't believe it, she told her daughter never to say that again, and never questioned the uncle. Several mistakes were made in this example. The mother was not bold enough to confront the uncle. Which implies she didn't have a voice herself and she hushed up too. The mother hushed her daughter, lost the communication and lost the chance to stop her child from being verbally sexually assaulted. We should always give the benefit of doubt to our children, especially in a situation involving molestation or sexual assault.

We must always talk to our kids about dangerous things people can do to them. If not, we will lose our kids to a lack of knowledge. Some parents may feel that some conversations are not needed based on their age. Not true. If a pedophile sees your child as a target, age is only intriguing, and never preventing. We must communicate.

2. Set Boundaries. We must explain to our children the importance of setting boundaries because they explore, develop, and contain more information faster, than our generation. For example, they need to know what is considered too close, and what they should

say if they feel someone is violating that boundary. We must also teach our kids that no hands go below their stomach, they have an invisible bubble around them and their body parts that must never be popped.

Here are some examples of a lack of boundaries: *The eight-year old daughter sits in a male's lap. The male may be an uncle, brother, dad, granddad, male coach, nephew.* The male body will react to anything that touches its genital area. Keep your sons and daughters out of guys' laps. I'm not saying do not let your kids hug Papa or Uncle Cool Bill, but again, be mindful that anything can trigger a pedophile. *The twelve-year old son wants to change into his swimming trunks beside the pool.* Your response should be, "No son, go to the bathroom or put a towel around you first." Setting and defining boundaries are a requirement.

3. Instill Boldness. My favorite defense is boldness. I love to teach boldness to a child because it creates a voice and protect our children. Quiet, shy, and timid individuals are more likely to be targeted because the pedophile sees weakness. We must instill a sense of boldness in children so that they will stand up against something that is not right and run off the pedophile.

I have seen adults who are not bold and do not have a voice. For example, I have seen a woman forced to eat something that she didn't like because she wasn't bold enough to say no. Imagine if someone close to you, approached your children, and asked them to perform something sexually or uncomfortable. Without knowledge and boldness, they may do it because they don't know what to say or be bold enough to say no.

I tell my girls often, to use their voice and never back down from something they believe is right or wrong. We must allow our kids to speak, and we must listen. When we don't allow them to speak, we miss out on valuable conversations and learning opportunities If we shut them up, they will remain silent when they should speak up.

I encourage my children to be bold in their conversations and responses, to people who put them in dangerous situations, or make them feel uncomfortable. I do this by providing them with strong and meaningful statements, that strike and oppose the intentions of the pedophile. My favorite funny line, that I use in my high pitch voice is, "Get your hands out of there." I say in a way that they will always remember it, and in a way that carries so much definition. I also tell them to be bold and intentional when saying, "Stay away," "I'll scream," "You should not be doing this," "You will get in a lot of trouble, once I tell my parents," and "Fire!" We must equip our children with words and phrases that are impactful, as well as, encourage them to be bold and fearless!

4. Instill Courage. I believe that courage combined with boldness, prevents our children from being molested. I see courage as a win against a pedophile, because our children will have the courage to defend themselves and to tell an adult when they are being mistreated. If children are courageous enough to defend themselves, then they will also have the courage to tell us. How do we do this? We do this by encouraging our children to win and encourage them to keep trying when they lose. We also do this by explaining the definition of courage, an empowering them to speak up during, "what if situations."

These situations are terrifying, horrific, and can become haunting long-term memories. We must be real with our children and teach them how to verbally defend themselves. I believe that vocal defense carries more than physical, because most pedophiles prey on the quiet. We beat this problem by giving our children the words to use and the courage to say no. We also beat this by teaching our children that it is courageous when they tell us what, who, and where. They must be reassured that we are courageous and that will do whatever it takes to protect them.

We love our children and must protect them. This is a requirement, because these horrific acts are continuing every day. Let's develop a sense of awareness, be concerned, and take every sign into consideration. We must provide protection for all children, because once it happens, recovery can take a lifetime. We must communicate with our children, set boundaries, and instill boldness and courage so that our children will win against the pedophile. Additionally, we must speak up and speak out to make a major difference in our world.

In conclusion, I am sharing my story to prevent child molestation from happening to other children. I feel that it's my mission to create open communication between parents and their children. So, I am providing parents the information they need to protect their child from molestation and sexual assault. This life mission has led to me sharing my story around the world, to help parents identify the risks and signs of molestation, and to encourage other childhood survivors to HUSH No More.

Jeremiah Anderson

Jeremiah is from Sanford, Florida. He is a strong leader in his community and a father of two daughters. His education includes, studies in meteorology, human sexuality, and physiology. Although Jeremiah never completed any of those degrees, he retained information that he uses currently as a community speaker. Jeremiah's favorite hobbies includes reading, writing, tracking weather phenomenon's, and improvising comedy. Jeremiah is a certified as a behavioral health care specialist and a motivational speaker who works with communities, activist groups, and individuals to create a better sense of how to cope and understand what we don't understand. Jeremiah believes that you can create your path by making better decisions daily. Jeremiah also believes that by spreading truth, we allow individuals to see the truth within themselves. Jeremiah supports the HUSH NO MORE movement because he understands that sexual abuse occurs in the most unexpected relationships. Jeremiah enjoys helping others and spreading kindness.

Which Child Sexual Abuse story impacted you the most?

_____

What did you learn about Child Sexual Abuse?

_____

_____

_____

List any additional thoughts you may have.

_____

_____

_____

_____

Sexual Harassment

Exposed

I Private Jones, in HHC 26th, Forward Support Battalion, states that my roommate, Private First Class Cooper, sexually harassed me in our barracks room. On 29 June, 1997, I was awakened by Private First Class Cooper climbing into bed with me after lights out. I laid very still as she cuddled up to me and whispered in my ear "This is professional development. Lesson one: spooning". She wrapped her arms around me and laid her head on my back. End of Statement.

Sergeant First Class Gray, read my statement and asked me, "Was that all she did?"

I replied, "Yes." He looked at my statement one more time and put it in the top drawer of his desk and said to me "Come back if anything else happens." His eyes were looking at the door as if that was my cue to leave. I left his office, feeling very sad and disappointed that he didn't say or do anything to Cooper. I also felt like he didn't take my sexual harassment complaint seriously.

When I got back to my room, I felt confused and mad because I thought Private First Class Cooper was my friend. When I had first gotten to the unit, she was responsible for showing me the ropes and she bought nice gifts. I didn't say anything to her from that day and vice versa. However, she continued to watch me and followed me around the post, as if she just happened to be at the same place as I was.

Months later, I realized that things had started changing at the dining facility, where I worked as a Cook. The entire dining facility staff started calling me names and harassing me because she had told everyone that I was gay and that I had approached her. I found all of this out when I was complaining to Specialist Ladson about how everyone was treating me. She said, "That's because you are gay and pushed up on Cooper." My mouth dropped open and I yelled "I am not gay! She is!" At that moment, I was pissed and determined to EXPOSE her.

I found Cooper and immediately started going off. I didn't care who heard me. I was so mad that I don't remember what I said. I only remember exposing her when she said, "After all I did for you, you are going to act like that towards me? Diss me like I'm one of those dudes chasing after you. I'm not going to chase you. All I wanted you to do was let me love you, treat you with" and before I realized it, I punched her in her mouth.

I couldn't even focus while she was talking, which is why I didn't notice that everyone had congregated around us, including the Command Sergeant Major (CSM) and the Battalion Commander (BC). These two were the most senior ranking soldiers in our organization and responsible for upholding the standards and enforcing the rules.

The CSM yelled, "Break it up! Both of you, and your Supervisor, meet us in the office now!" I was so mad that I didn't even care. I marched right into their office, ready to explain my side of the story by continuing to expose Cooper.

"So, explain to us, how did we get here today?" asked the CSM.

I yelled, "She is fucking lying on me!" The CSM told me to watch my mouth and explain.

"It all started when I first arrived. She was my roommate. Her and her boyfriend took me under their wings. I didn't have a car or much money, and they made sure I had everything I needed. We were like the Three Musketeers. I went everywhere and did everything with them. The problem came when PFC Cooper climbed into bed with me and whispered in my ear, "This is professional developed. Lesson one: spooning." The BC took a deep breath and put his arms behind his head and leaned back in his chair. After he let out a dramatic sigh, he said, "We are here this evening, wasting valuable time about spooning?"

SFC Gray, my Supervisor, cleared his voice and said, "Sir, can I chime in on the issue?" The BC nodded. SFC Gray continued by saying. "A few months ago, Private Jones came to me about the problem she was having with PFC Cooper and the 'spooning incident." I was going to have their room assignments changed, but instead, I put the soldiers on opposite work shifts. I assumed the problem had died down, because I didn't hear any more about it until today. Apparently, the move only heightened Private First Class Cooper's obsession with Private Jones and it began to spill over to the workplace and resulted in the argument that occurred today."

The BC leaned over and looked me sternly in my eyes and said, "I am disappointed in you! You have done remarkable things by being recognized as the Soldier of the Quarter, and your leaders all have such wonderful things to say about you. Why did you result to physically attacking PFC Cooper?" I responded by saying, "I was just fed up with her! She was always watching me, peering at me, and talking about me. She told lies about me. She has everyone believing that I was the homosexual and that I made a pass at her when it was her all along.

After Specialist Ladson told me about her lies, I walked into the Dining Facility Kitchen. There she was smirking at me. The next thing I knew, the CSM was yelling for us to stop." Cooper was just sitting there holding her mouth and looking at the floor the entire time that I was talking.

The BC rested his face in his hand. He seemed pretty stumped like he didn't know the right thing to say or do. He then turned the conversation back to SFC Gray.

"SFC Gray, I do think that you tried to handle this situation. However, we as leaders have to take it more seriously. Sexual Harassment is not tolerated by either sex. When someone is being harassed it takes them out of their character. We are lucky that all we had is this incident." He turned and focused on me and said, "It is understandable why you reacted the way that you did, but it's not acceptable behavior."

He switched his focus to all three of us and said, "All three of you will provide a training modular on Sexual Harassment that will be presented to the Battalion for training. SFC Gray, you will address how to react to sexual harassment from a leader perspective. Private Jones, you will discuss actions to take when being sexually harassed. PFC Cooper, you will discuss the dangers of harassing and the consequences. I look forward to the training on Thursday. You are all dismissed."

While serving in the United States Army as a Noncommissioned Officer and a Commissioned Officer, I have witnessed individuals who have been victims of the HUSH Topics. I wrote this story based on one of the events that occurred in my organization. So often, supervisors fail to handle sexual assault and sexual harassment complaints properly, and at times, they do not properly handle LGBTQ incidents as well. I hope this story brings more awareness to the HUSH Topics.

*The names in this story has been changed to protect the identity of all involved in this hostile work environment.

LeDesma Terry's biography is shared under her Domestic Violence stories.

How did this Sexual Harassment story impact you?

_____

What did you learn about Sexual Harassment?

_____

_____

_____

_____

List any additional thoughts you may have.

_____

_____

_____

_____

Sex Trafficking

Superstar

Ten years ago, I was a vibrant and smart seventh grader, who was on the honor roll and loved being a cheerleader. Unlike most of my friends, my parents were happily married and provided everything that my two brothers and I needed. I felt loved and spoiled because I was the baby girl. I imagined going to college to become a marine biologist, getting married to a prince, having two children, and living by the ocean so that I could study the life span of whales and dolphins. I never imagined that my life would turn into a horror movie that starred me and so many men that I can't count.

I loved going to school because I was able to learn about the world and spend time with my friends. All of my teachers loved me, especially my science teacher/assistant football coach, Mr. Howard. Mr. Howard was about thirty years old, funny and cool. He was my favorite teacher because he always told me how I had a bright future and that I was smart, pretty, and a superstar. I would help him after school by grading papers when I didn't have cheerleading practice. I loved helping him because he told the best stories and always had candy and soda in his classroom. His stories turned into my personal adventures that I couldn't wait to do. One day, he asked me if I wanted to attend an exclusive science convention with him. I was excited because I was the only one that he thought was mature and smart enough to go. He said that I couldn't tell anyone because I was not old enough to attend, but that he would give me a fake ID to get in.

I had never told my parents a "big" lie before, but I knew I could pull it off. I came up with a plan to tell them that I was going to a cheerleading convention with Coach Carrie and would be gone all day. My mom dropped me off at the school, where I met Mr. Howard. He was so excited to see me. We left in his black convertible Mercedes, with dark tinted windows and black leather seats. I remember feeling like a princess riding in the front seat, while he played jazz music. We talked, laughed, and stopped to eat at a beautiful Italian restaurant, before heading to the science convention. I was a little disappointed when he got an emergency call from who I thought was his brother. His brother called and said that he needed him to pick him up from jail for speeding. Since I wasn't supposed to be with him; he asked me if I would go to his sister Amanda's house and wait for him. We pulled up to her house, and I couldn't wait to go in. Ms. Amanda's house was so pretty and perfectly decorated. I introduced myself and told her that

I couldn't wait to have a house of my own. Mr. Howard left me and promised to return, but he never did.

Ms. Amanda was beautiful and very nice. She told me that I was gorgeous and should be a model. I had never thought about being a model until she told me that she had traveled the world and made a lot of money modeling clothes and jewelry. Instantly, I wanted to be a model. She took pictures of me and showed me how to walk, pose, and look seductive. Ms. Amanda became my big sister in a matter of hours, and I trusted everything that she said and told me to do. She called Christopher, her agent, and begged him to come see me. When Mr. Christopher came, I was very nervous because I didn't think that I was as pretty as Ms. Amanda. He saw me and said, "I am going to make you into a superstar!" I loved that idea because Mr. Howard always called me "Superstar."

While waiting on Mr. Howard, I must have fallen asleep. When I woke up, I had a headache, and I had never been to this place before. I was in a small room that had a queen-sized bed, covered with a pink unicorn comforter set. I felt scared because the door was locked and there were no windows, only a nightstand with a small lamp. The walls were painted a washed-out pink and a small silver pot was in the corner. I started crying and banging on the door for my mom and dad. I was so scared. After about an hour Mr. Christopher came in and gave me the rules that would change my life forever. He looked me dead into my soul and said, "Unfortunately, Mr. Howard killed your family, so I'm your daddy now. As long as you follow my rules, I will take care of you and love you forever." I heard him, but I didn't hear him. It was like I was living outside of my body, watching him tell a little girl this, but it wasn't me.

The five rules were:

1. Listen and do what I say
2. Never believe or listen to anyone else
3. Always tell the truth
4. Never steal
5. Remember the rules

The next day, Ms. Amanda came and put my hair into two ponytails and gave me a school uniform to put on. She said that if I followed the rules and made everyone happy that one day, I could buy a house just like hers. I started crying, and she gently covered my mouth with her left hand and wiped my tears with her right hand. Then she said, "Never let anyone see you cry. They will think you are weak, and they will never stop. Trust me. You will survive because I did." Every day for seven years, I remembered her advice. I never saw Ms. Amanda again. However, I always wonder what happened to her because she was the only one that cared for me, although, I get mad at her for not helping me escape.

Hours after Ms. Amanda left, Daddy came in with a big smile. He said, "Superstar, I have good news. I have a friend that wants to meet you. Be nice and do what he says." I was nervous but anxious to meet this new friend. Shortly afterward, a man entered the pink room. I will never forget how he looked at me as if I was fresh meat. He was a little taller than me, with a bald shiny head, wide shoulders, and big hands that seem to consume my entire body. He came over to the bed and said, "Are you a virgin?" I shook my head yes. He replied, "Good because I paid good money for you." I was so confused and scared because I knew that he was going to have sex with me.

I don't remember anything else about the first time. I guess I blocked the horrific event in my brain. Unfortunately, I remember everything about the 300 plus men and 100 plus women I have been with over the years. I remember their smell, touch, facial hair, chest hair, pubic hair, smiles, stares, penis size, vagina size and if they wore a wedding ring. I remember the hotel rooms, houses, and abandoned buildings where my body was a playground, and every hole on my body that was used for their pleasure.

Daddy made sure that no one ever hurt me. He was my protector, my only friend, my advisor, my confidant, and my teacher because I never went back to school. It was me and him against the world. I was his Superstar and daughter. I know some of you are wondering how I could feel this way about him. Well, it's simple. He provided for me and ensured that I had everything I could possibly need. Yes, he was a Sex Trafficker, but I never even knew what sex trafficking was.

My life changed when I turned twenty-one. My daddy had a heart attack and was rushed to the hospital in an ambulance. Once I got to the hospital and tried to check-in, they told me that he had died in the ambulance. All I remember is dropping to my knees and crying loudly in the lobby. I felt someone put their hand on my shoulder and whispered in my ear. "Baby, I will be here with you as long as you need me." Nurse Sheila was a short and petite lady, with dark chocolate skin and a short afro. Her eyes were light brown and seemed to stare into my soul. I immediately trusted her and allowed her to comfort me at the worst time of my life. I confided in her that my family had been killed and that my dad was all I had left. She said, "Mr. _____ was your dad? We assumed that he was your pimp." I was in shock and mad that they could think that about my dad. I went on to tell her how wrong she was, and how he had taken care of me when I had no one else. Nurse Sheila told me that my dad was an evil man, who had been known for beating women and forcing them to have sex with men for money. She pulled out her cell phone and showed me a mug shot of my dad to prove her story. I immediately started crying again because I knew that she was telling the truth.

Soon afterward, the police came and took me to the police station, where they questioned me for hours. They told me how my family had been looking for me and thought that I had run away or was dead. I felt numb and ashamed because I was not the same little girl they had been searching for. I begged the detective not to contact my parents; he didn't listen. My family came to the police station looking for their little girl. Instead, they found a grown woman, who was grieving for the man that was her new dad and only friend. My brothers, mom, and dad all hugged me in a big circle, but I really didn't want to see them. I can't explain how seeing them made me feel. I guess I had thought that they were dead for so long that I didn't think they were real. Everything seemed like a dream.

I went home with them and entered my old room. It looked exactly the same, my cheerleading pictures were on the wall, my dolls and bears were neatly on my bed as if they were waiting for me to come home. I felt very detached as if my room was a museum. I didn't want to be there, but I had no place else to go. My family tried their best to make me feel comfortable. They were very nice and did everything they could to adjust their schedule to ensure that someone was always at home with me. As I look back, I am sure that they were just as scared as I was.

Today, after years of therapy and family therapy I am doing a lot better. I go to counseling twice a week and I work at the Boys and Girls Club. I still have dreams about my "Daddy," but thankfully it's not every night. I still live at home with my parents because I am fearful of living on my own, trusting people, and of running into one of the many men and women I allowed to use my body. I am still trying to work this out with my counselor.

I don't know if I will ever be able to live a normal life, however, I try very hard. My counselor told me about the HUSH No More project and introduced me to Dr. Guyton. After speaking with her, I decided to share my story for two reasons: 1. Parents and children need to be aware of the risks of their children being taken. 2. I had no idea what Sex Trafficking was, and I assume that others do not know either, so this is a way to inform everyone. I have decided not to share my name because I am still trying to figure out my future. I am not sure if I want my real name associated with sex trafficking because society will see me as a whore, since I never tried to leave or fight back. I am hoping that my story will change the opinion of so many women and men like me. If you are in a similar situation, please know that there are a lot of people who are willing to help. Over the years, I have met many of them and have participated in their programs. Remember that you are never alone because God is always watching over you, even when you don't think so. He eventually brought me home to the family that loves me despite the word "Sex Trafficking."

My advice to young girls and boys:

1. Don't trust anyone that makes you feel uncomfortable or touches you in your private spots.
2. Don't trust any adult that you have to lie to your parents to be around.
3. When your gut tells you that something is wrong, believe it, and get out of the situation safely.
4. Don't think that you are untouchable and can never end up in the sex trafficking community.
5. Learn all you can learn about predators and sex trafficking. The more you know, the less likely you will become a victim.

My advice to parents:

1. Talk to your children about sex and predators at an early age.
2. Don't tell your children that you will kill anyone that hurts them because they will be scared to tell.
3. Don't trust anyone around your kids, this includes teachers, coaches, priest, pastors, neighbors, etc.

4. Always pop up unannounced if your children are spending time away from you.
5. Encourage a trusting relationship with a family or friend that you trust who your child can talk to about anything. We never told our parents everything; don't expect your children to tell you everything.
6. Don't underestimate a predator. They can ham your children.
7. Be vigilant, become informed, and attend local community events.

The author is currently attending college in Florida, majoring in Child Psychology. Her goal is to work with abducted and abused children. She enjoys learning, completing puzzles, and volunteering at her local shelter. One day she hopes to inspire the world to be more kind and loving.

How did this Sex Trafficking story impact you?

_____

What did you learn about Sex Trafficking?

_____

_____

_____

List any additional thoughts you may have.

_____

_____

_____

_____

Dr. Guyton's Right to Tell It

R. Kelly

What is your favorite R Kelly song or CD?

Most people love his music and know every beat.

Not me...because when I hear his voice, I remember the day when you asked me to go to dinner and treated me like a queen.

You were so nice, and I didn't think you could ever be evil. That is why I trusted you when you said "Lets go to my room to watch a movie."

Your dark arms turned into snakes as they started to explore my body.

They were strong and overpowered my small hands. Your couch turned into a bed as you pushed me down. You took your pants down, faster than a speed of light.

I couldn't believe that you were entering my treasure, for only your pleasure.

I just laid there, with questions running through my head. Why are you doing this? Why are you hurting me? Are you wearing a condom? Will I catch AIDS? Will I get pregnant? Will you ever stop? I became lost in my thoughts as you took over my body without permission. I just laid there not fighting back with salty tears falling down my face. It was like you were running a race.

When I tuned out your heavy breathing, all I could hear was

"I don't see nothing wrong with a little bump n grind"

"Homie Lover Friend"

"It seems like you're ready"

"Sex me," and finally

"12 Play."

You raped me for the entire CD, as if it was your theme song and hours long.

So yes, I hate the sound of R Kelly's voice and the sound of your voice as you said, "Soldier, no one will believe you."

Private Vanessa Dunn

*This poem was written to allow myself to heal and to stop my mind from racing.

When a Date Turns to Rape

One of the hardest decisions I ever had to make mentally was to allow myself to remember being sexually assaulted on February 14, 1994, in Schweinfurt, Germany. It took fifteen years for me to even acknowledge that it had happened. I am assuming that this was my way of protecting myself from the hurt, pain, embarrassment, frustration, guilt, self-blame, anger, and fear. I may have forgotten, but my actions and behaviors never forgot. What I mean by this is, I have made a lot of bad decisions as they related to relationships. I invite you to come on this journey with me as I tell you what has happened in my life, as a result of being violated by someone I trusted and admired.

Living My Best Life

I was a nineteen-year old Private, serving in the United States Army, in Schweinfurt, Germany, my first duty stationed as the Post Commander Secretary. This was a very prestigious position and was held normally by a Sergeant. Like most teenagers, I thought I knew everything and called most people that I met my friend. Now, as I look back, I realize that I was very naïve about men and friendships. I attribute most of that to growing up in the church and not being able to date (with permission). My mother believed that if she kept us in church, that we wouldn't get into trouble. Overall, I was a good girl, but I did have three boyfriends before joining the Army. When I joined the Army, I felt like I was free to make my own decisions, and essentially, to do what I thought I was grown enough to do. That included going out on dates, having my first drink, and cursing. Something that my mom would have cringed at, but I knew she would love me regardless.

The military base in Schweinfurt, Germany, had very few female soldiers. There were only five women on the entire post, and three of us were African American. That being known, we were sexually harassed often and were asked on dates almost every day. At first, I wouldn't go out on any dates because I was focused on school and just trying to make it through my two-year assignment. Eventually, I got extremely bored and started accepting some of the offers for dinner. I learned quickly that it had nothing to do with my vibrant personality and smile, but for my private goodies. I learned even faster how to kindly turn men down or ignore them if they were rude and disrespectful. I thought that I was good at judging character and could tell if someone was full of crap. Even times that I couldn't figure them out, my roommate and I would compare notes on who tried to talk to us, and if we'd seen them displaying some type of negative behavior. Our girl talks after work would be very interesting and led to us believing that we had a good system in place to judge men.

I would also ask the opinion of my mentor, Staff Sergeant Joseph. He was about thirty years old, high speed, and the Post Commander's Driver. He would mentor me about life, the military, being promoted, men, and how to carry myself as a young lady. He was like a wise big brother, who had a lot of experience. We would talk for hours, on days that the senior leadership was out of the office. He was not my supervisor, but he took me under his wing. Although, I had my system in place, it wasn't foolproof.

A couple of weeks before Valentine's Day, a very handsome Staff Sergeant, asked me if I wanted to get out of the barracks and have dinner. I said yes, because he was in his early thirties, a cool Infantryman, respectful, and talked to me like I was his sister. Most of the guys my age were arrogant at times or just rude. In my mind, this was something different and hopefully would turn into a cool friendship. I definitely thought he was too old to even consider him as a boyfriend. Our first time hanging out, we went to a Chinese restaurant right outside of the post. We talked about the military, history, college, family, and all subjects in between. I thought he was smart, funny, and very nice. He also talked to me about my military career and what I needed to do to be promoted. After that first night, we started hanging out at the bowling alley. He was very respectful and never gave me any indication that he looked at me more than a sister. That is why when he asked me to go out to dinner on Valentine's Day, I thought it would be like the rest of the times that we hung out. Staff Sergeant Joseph asked me what I was doing for Valentine's Day. I told him about Staff Sergeant Infantryman, and that we were going to hangout. Staff Sergeant Joseph immediately warned me to be careful because Staff Sergeant Infantryman was a womanizer. I laughed it off and told him that we were just friends and that I trusted him. Essentially, I did not listen to my mentor.

Life-Changing

On February 14, 1994, at approximately 1800 hours, (6:00 PM), Staff Sergeant Infantryman met me in front of my barracks, and together we walked to a small German restaurant right outside of the gate. We picked there because we knew that the nice restaurants would be very busy. Dinner was cool and full of laughter. Unlike in the States, the drinking age was eighteen, so I happily accepted the three glasses of wine. The night was going great, so when he suggested that we go back to his barracks room to watch some *In Living Color* VCR tapes, that his brother had sent him from the States, I said yes. It was still early, and I didn't have anything else to do. We walked to his room, and I sat on his couch, while he started up the VCR player. Soon, I started laughing at Fire Marshall Bill, Nosey Wanda, and the many characters that the Wayans brothers had created. After we had watched all of the shows, he said, "Do you want to hear the new R. Kelly CD, I bought?" I wanted to hear it because I had only heard two of the songs, and R Kelly was really popular. Once he popped in the CD, I was impressed at his setup, because he had an entire sound system in his room, unlike the little boom box I had. You could feel the base and probably hear his music all the way down the hall. As I reflect, he probably wanted the music to be loud so no one would hear the horrible events taking place in his room.

After starting the CD player, he came and sat back down next to me on the couch. I don't know if it was my intuition, but things seemed different. He made eye contact with me like a man makes contact with a woman that he desires. I laughed and said, "Why are you looking at me like that?" He said, "Because you are beautiful, and I have wanted you since the first time I saw you." I thought he was joking, but when he leaned in to kiss me, I knew he wasn't. Before I could process the moment, his mouth was on mine. I tried to push him off, but I swear he was strong as Hulk Hogan. He pulled back, which gave me time to say, "I just want to be friends." He replied, "I know you want me, I see the way you look at me." Before I could get up, it was like his couched turned into a bed. I tried to push him off, but his arms wrapped around me like a boa constrictor, and his eyes turned into two black coals, and the smile that was always there, disappeared. I just laid there as he held me down with his left forearm, while pinning my legs with his legs, and using his right hand to remove my underwear. I don't know why I didn't scream. It was as if I had an out-of-body experience. I could see him taking my soul away, but I didn't know what to do. In the Army, you are trained to fight and go to war. For some reason, at this moment, I realized that the military didn't train me for this battle. I was NOT prepared to experience the forcefulness of a penis inside of me. I was NOT prepared for him to act like this violation was a consented agreement. I was NOT prepared for his sweat to drip all over my body and face. I was NOT prepared for him to ejaculate inside of my hidden treasure as if it was his secret land to deposit his disgusting sperm. I WAS NOT PREPARED.

Weirdly, while he was "handling his business," I focused on the 12 Play CD being played for my listening pleasure. All I could hear was "I don't see nothing wrong with a little bump n grind." "Homie Lover Friend," "It seems like you're ready" "Sex Me" and finally "12 Play." I wanted to escape the moment as if it wasn't happening. However, I was unsuccessful because my mind was on its on personal racetrack of questions. "Why was he doing this to me?" "Did I give him a sign that I wanted this?" "Was he wearing a condom?" "Will I catch AIDS?" "Will I get pregnant?" "Will he ever stop hurting me?" I had no answers, only tears that I thought would have given him an indication that I did not want him…but I was wrong. Twenty-four years later, I can still smell his Obsession cologne mixed with his disgusting sweat.

Once he was done, and slowly eased out of me, he kissed me on my right cheek and said, in his deep raspy voice, "Soldier, no one will believe you." I turned my face in disgust and hatred because I knew he was right. Who would believe a Private who willingly came to his room after dinner? I quickly got dressed and slammed the door as I left his room for the first and last time. As I was walking in the dark to my room, I felt so stupid, used, hurt, and scared. I had no idea what to do. As soon I got to my room, I immediately took a shower to attempt to erase his smell, sweat, and semen off of my body. I threw my outfit in the trash because I never wanted to be reminded of that night again. I thought I could wash that entire night away, as if it never happened. All night, I felt like he would come to my room to talk to me, so I moved the nightstand to barricade my door. My roommate asked me what I was doing, and I told her that I thought I saw some crazy guys outside of our building. Fortunately, he never came, but I could hear footsteps all night. I couldn't sleep because every time I closed my eyes, I would see him smiling at me. When the sun began to rise, I made a promise to myself that I wouldn't let him control my thoughts or my body ever again.

The next day, I went to Physical Training, which is the Army's version of exercise, as if nothing ever happened. I hated running, but for some reason, I couldn't wait to run to let my body and mind escape the bad thoughts. I went to work and smiled as if I had no worries in my life. When Staff Sergeant Joseph asked me how my night was, I lied and said, "We had a good time and our food was good." I felt so bad lying to him. However, there was no way that I could tell him what happened. I knew that if I told him, he would probably hurt the Infantryman. The last thing I wanted was for him to get into trouble because of my dumb mistake.

Effects of the Rape

After this event, my life changed. It was as if I started living three different lives. There was the Private Dunn, Vanessa, and Latrice. All three of my personalities lived distinct lives, without acknowledging the event. I didn't even realize that this was happening. I only acknowledged this change about four years ago when a friend of mine was talking about her depression and being diagnosed with Borderline Personality Disorder. I looked up the definition and knew this diagnosis explained me. I was excited to finally explain how I was feeling in the inside, but also sad that I had a mental disorder. Below is a short description of each person living inside of me.

Private Dunn worked hard, smiled, and focused on college so she could be promoted and eventually get out of the Army. Physically, she struggled in the Army. She started gaining weight and had a hard time passing her Physical Training Test. She felt like if she gained weight, Soldiers wouldn't be physically attracted to her. She was wrong because the more weight she gained, the shapelier she became, and men sexually harassed her even more. No one in her leadership noticed the change in her demeanor or uniform. Maybe they didn't know how to approach her, or they were too busy to notice. Regardless, she felt all alone. She wanted to get out of the military because she found it hard to trust her Brothers in Arms. However, the military was good for her financially and was paying for a good college education. She loved her job and enjoyed taking care of soldiers. She wasn't good at the physical aspects of the military, but she knew the regulations and became a subject matter expert that her leadership relied on. After ten years, she was financially stable, finished her MBA, and received an honorable discharge from the military. This led to her being able to maintain her standard of living and be able to transition into being a government employee, with the same smile, and same work ethics.

Vanessa smiled all of the time. She was respectful, caring, and would give her last to help anyone in need. She would volunteer in her community by feeding the homeless, mentoring youth, and at church.

Mostly, she focused on others, so she didn't have to focus on herself. Somehow, God blessed her to find a husband that was loving and patient. Together they had a blended family of five children, whom she loved dearly. She found it hard to be the mother she thought they deserved but did everything she could for them. She was a hardworking government employee, that got along with all of her supervisors and co-workers. She also started her own business, Consulting Experts & Associates, LLC. Regardless of her mental instability, she finished her doctoral degree in seven years instead of four. In contrast, Vanessa suffered from major depression. There were days that she couldn't get out of the bed, and she cried all the time for no reason. She was a functional and productive alcoholic, that drank almost every day, for over ten years. She was hyper vigilant and checked windows and doors, while finding it hard to sleep without the TV on. The desire for sex was nonexistent because she didn't feel sexy, only dirty. Her mental health was a secret that only a few close family and friends knew about. She went to the VA, but most of the time, all they would do is prescribe medications and offer counseling, which in her mind was not a true solution. She lived in denial about what had happened to her and waited years, before she was able to recall her sexual assault to start a journey of survival and healing.

Latrice was a charismatic manipulator. She hated men and vowed to never let another one hurt her again. She found herself in noncommittal relationships with married men and single men because she didn't value herself and thought that all men only wanted sex. She would get drunk before having sex and intentionally placed herself in situations that could have led to another sexual assault, because she felt like if it happened again she would respond differently and hurt the man that attempted to rape her. Fortunately, it never happened again, but in her mind, she was waiting for the day it would. Latrice found it hard to be married, because she didn't believe that he really loved her or that she could meet his needs. There is a saying that "Hurt people, hurt people;" Latrice was proof of this saying. Thankfully, her husband loved her through it all and dedicated his life to being her best friend, even after their divorce.

During this difficult time of my life, I was asked to be an Instructor for the U.S. Army's Sexual Assault and Harassment Program. This position required me to train and credential Victim Advocates and Sexual Response Coordinators who would be responsible for assisting Victims of Military Sexual Trauma. I believe that God works in mysterious ways, because I never had any intentions on being a Victim Advocate, much less training them. I feel like it was God's way of making me help a population that would lead to me understanding victimology and how I was a victim as well. I still did not remember my sexual assault, while providing sexual assault training, I just thought I was a very caring and passionate Instructor.

Memory Recall

After fifteen years of suppressing my rape, a significant event occurred that triggered my memory. I was walking in the Columbia Mall and I could have sworn that I saw the Infantryman coming out of a men's store. The man walked just like him and had the same complexion. At that moment, I instantly froze and started sweating and feeling like the day that he raped me. In that moment, I became one person, as my memory started returning. I can't really explain how I started living one life, that included disgust, fear, suicidal ideations and anxiety. By this time, I was divorced, my children were grown, and I lived all alone. I couldn't sleep because I felt like he would come into my room and rape me all over again. All night I kept checking my alarm system and made sure that my gun was loaded and on my nightstand. For approximately three months, I rarely slept because my mind would be racing about him, or I would have a flashback when I closed my eyes. I was a zombie at work, but I kept a smile on my face and pretended that I wasn't suffering mentally. I didn't tell anyone because I was embarrassed that this man still had control of my life. I hated him and wanted him eliminated from this Earth.

Ironically, I still do not remember everything about that night. I don't even remember his real name, which is why I call him Staff Sergeant Infantryman. Sometimes, his face will flash before my eyes. Sometimes, I remember walking home by myself, but never is there a complete picture of the night I was rapped. The brain has a way of protecting itself from trauma. I often joke that I suffer from CRS (Can't Remember Shit). However, after years of looking for an answer to this strange phenomenon, I found research that explains why so many victims like myself have high rates of memory loss.

In 2016, the *Guardian*, a news organization, published research on repressed memory loss and explained how the suppression of memories is linked to a decrease in activity in the hippocampus, the area of the brain involved with making new memories and retrieving old ones. Essentially, your brain will forget memories that you don't want, but in doing this, it makes your brain ineffective for future memories. I really want society to understand this research, so they can stop saying things like, "Why did they wait so long before coming forward?" "That happened a long time ago." "They must be lying since they never told anyone." The truth is, coming forward is one of the hardest things that a person will ever do in their lifetime, especially if the memory is suppressed.

Getting Help

Finally, I found the courage and desire to go seek help, after being forcibly admitted into the Dorn VA Hospital in Columbia, South Carolina. One day, I had gotten so drunk that I couldn't stop crying for approximately six hours. I called my sister-friend, LaTasha, and she came and drove me to the VA. When I arrived, I was so drunk and depressed that the emergency room doctor couldn't admit me until my alcohol level had decreased. I was admitted into the hospital for detox and extensive counseling for five days. This was the best thing that could have happened to me, because I was able to detach myself from the world and focus on myself. While there, I told my psychiatrist about my Military Sexual Trauma (MST). After expressing this to him, he suggested that I receive counseling at the Vet Center. I had participated in counseling with about twenty other counselors, but none of them understood me. The Vet Center was a game-changer for me. There I met Ms. Price, a beautiful counselor with a beautiful spirit. She was the first one that I trusted and gave me good advice. I was able to talk to her about my assault and discussed strategies to overcome the negative and fearful thoughts in my mind. I started writing about my feelings and my thoughts about how I viewed myself. I imagined that she would flinch when I told her about all of the men I had slept with and hurt...but she just listened without any judgment and helped me to remove the negative relationships from my life. Every session included me coming up with a strategy to increase my self-worth, to live a true and authentic life, and to eliminate the negative thoughts about myself, men, and the Infantryman.

Today, I am still in counseling and consider it as part of my self-care. I don't cry as often, but I do release all of the negativity that occurs in my life and I leave it in her office. Ms. Price is absolutely wonderful and saved my life. There is a stigma associated with counseling. However, I genuinely believe that it's an essential part of recovery. I want you to understand that counseling is priceless and is a significant part of my ability to heal and unleash the shame.

Counseling is a major part of my life. However, I have implemented the following healing modalities and strategies: Tell myself that I AM A SURVIVOR. Meditate to align my chakras (I started with guided videos from YouTube). Say a prayer of thanks every morning to start my day out with a positive outlook. Rearrange my house so that it feels safe and relaxing. Burn incense and essential oils daily. Use crystals and stones to help with my depression and to block negative energy (amethyst and obsidian are my favorite). Remove negative friends and family members from my inner circle who were not supportive. Add positive friends to my inner circle who support my journey. Attend AA meetings for support and encouragement. Listen to positive videos on YouTube for motivation. Speak and believe positive words of affirmations. Journal about how I currently feel and about my future. Color in an adult coloring book to relax. Volunteer at the homeless shelter and created the HUSH No More organization to support other victims and survivors to help them heal. All of these strategies have helped me heal. They may or may not work for everyone, but they are a good start.

I am no longer drinking, and I can proudly say that I attend *Spiritual Progress* a women's only Alcoholics Anonymous (AA) group in Columbia, South Carolina. These ladies have changed my life because they love me because I am a recovering alcoholic and have shared their personal experiences to encourage me on this journey. Alcohol is a depressant and will make you feel good and forget the bad thoughts in your head temporarily. However, when you sober up, you feel worse, so you start drinking again. It's a vicious cycle that is hard to get out of, but it's possible.

On this new sober journey, I have learned that if you have mental illness or a family history of alcoholism, alcohol can multiply your symptoms. At first, I was embarrassed about my drinking problem.

Attending AA changed this mindset, because there are all types of people in AA who are struggling just like me (doctors, lawyers, nurses, rich people, poor people, Christians, Catholics, Atheists, Muslims, all races, young and old). Nobody is exempt from alcoholism. Now, I am proud, because many people don't have the courage or the strength to stop drinking, but I do. If you determine that you have a problem, always remember that there is FREE help available www.aa.org

Living My NEW Best Life as Dr. Vanessa Dunn Guyton

I am grateful to write that I am no longer living my life as three distinct personalities. I feel like I am one whole person, who still suffers from depression, but strives to have more good days than bad. I have a genuine smile, and I make healthy decisions when it comes to men and my overall health. This all happened after counseling, prayer, and acknowledging the problems. Surprisingly, after years of living in shame and letting one event change my life, I decided to be proactive and stop allowing my rape to affect my future and to dedicate my life to helping victims of trauma. I also decided that I had NO reason to feel ashamed. The Infantryman should be the one who is living in shame for what he did to me.

When I decided to take my life back and to become a thriving Survivor, God started revealing ideas to me that would forever change my life. The first idea came while I was in a strategy session with my Life Coach, Angela Carr Patterson. We discussed how I could tackle the problems that many victims face, by using my experience as a Training Instructor and by sharing the stories of Survivors. That day, the HUSH No More Movement was created. We started planning training, speaking engagements, the documentary, and the book you are currently reading. Although, I had worked with Angela for years, I never told her that I was a Survivor, until she asked me directly while we were filming the documentary. Once, I told her, the ideas started to flow. She told me that I had to become the face of the organization and share my story to help others. At first, I was scared, but I prayed and released that fear to my Creator.

On February 8, 2019, I was attending a spiritual retreat in Charlotte, North Carolina. During this retreat, God told me to turn HUSH No More into a nonprofit organization. I have heard people talking about hearing from God, but it had never happened to me until this day. I clearly saw HUSH No More serving the world, to eliminate the HUSH Topics and providing money to assist in providing training to churches, communities, and nonprofit organizations that could not afford to pay for services. I also met my spiritual mothers, Momma Mildred Blakeny and Momma Mae Milloy, who started encouraging me. I had finally understood my purpose and knew that it was to create ways to protect God's people from becoming victims and to assist those who already were. I am so humbled and grateful that I have been charged with this mission because I now can turn what was meant to harm me into something beautiful.

People often ask me, how I overcame my rape. The truth is, it's something that you never "get over." You find healthy ways to deal with the memory, find a great support system, make safer decisions, and focus on taking your power back to live a higher quality of life. I pray that my decision to HUSH No More will encourage you to do the same, and or support others who have been through significant trauma in their life.

I am pretty sure that some people will judge me for sharing my story and the decisions that I have made in my life, but I no longer care. I am finally at a point in MY life that I will no longer hide my truth but share it to prevent others from living a similar journey. I pray that one day, society will punish the offender instead of the victim and that there will be more support systems for men and women, like myself. I also pray that you are encouraged by my writing and that you will find value in your life to bravely face another day.

My Daily Affirmations

I Am Smart.

I Am Kind.

I AM Beautiful.

I Am Important.

I AM Talented.

I AM the Leader of MY Family.

Created by my daughter, Teaira Mack.

*Staff Sergeant Joseph's name has been changed to protect his identity.

Source:

https://www.theguardian.com/science/2016/mar/15/suppressing-traumatic-memories-can-cause-amnesia-research-suggests

Dr. Vanessa Guyton

Dr. Vanessa Dunn Guyton is a Survivor of Military Sexual Trauma who is also a champion for Victims and Survivors all over the world. She truly believes that her purpose in life, is to bring awareness to God's people that will protect them from becoming a Victim of the HUSH Topics. Her goal is to provide workshops that help victims Unleash the Shame to Heal. Dr. Guyton enjoys learning, eating good food, visiting beaches, and traveling all around the world to experience various cultures. Contact her on social media or email her at admin@thehushtopics.com for speaking engagements and training.

How did Dr. Guyton's story impact you?

_____

What did you learn from her story?

_____

_____

_____

_____

List any additional thoughts you may have.

_____

_____

_____

Support/ Words of Encouragement

After experiencing trauma, we must remember that our lives are not over. For this reason, we all need to find a healthy way to adopt a lifestyle that includes progress, growth, and elevation. One of the hardest things to do is to live a healthy lifestyle that includes exercise, sleep, good eating habits, spiritual practices, and emotional well-being. Finding the courage to motivate and encourage ourselves, during those difficult times, is part of living a healthy life. Research has shown that speaking positive words to yourself, on a daily basis, can improve your mood, improve your interactions with others, and increase your overall outlook on life. Below are two affirmations that you can use to include positivity in your life and to prevent those negative ideas from consuming your mind. Always remember that YOU ARE NOT YOUR TRAUMA; YOU ARE A SURVIVOR.

Survivor's Pledge

I am a Victorious Survivor.

If peace can be had, I will find it.

If meaning and purpose can be made, I will make it.

If redemption can be done, I will do it.

If life can be lived, I will live it.

I will stand tall, I will breathe deep, and I will love and honor myself without shame or stigma.

I will learn to love, laugh, and relax, as best I am able, so to speed my healing now that the danger has passed.

I survived. I will thrive. I will be a Victorious Survivor.

Bill Jenkins

A Meditation for Survivors

Right now, in this place, in this time, I am safe.

All danger is over. All trauma has passed.

There is no shame in being overpowered by stronger forces. There is no guilt in being an innocent victim.

I survived. I faced death and walked away alive.

My invisible scars remind me of my victory.

I belong here. I will stand tall. I will breathe deep.

I am grateful for my life and purpose.

I am grateful for those who love and support me.

I know they are grateful that I am here.

I am grateful I survived. I am a victor not a victim.

All danger is over. All trauma has passed.

I will live, I will thrive, I will be safe.

Bill Jenkins

Bill Jenkins

Taking what he learned first-hand in the aftermath of his son's murder in 1997, Bill Jenkins wrote and self-published *What to do When the Police Leave: A Guide to the First Days of Traumatic Loss*. This landmark book on grief and bereavement quickly became an important resource for families dealing with the sudden or traumatic death of a loved one and the caregivers who work with them. He has received many awards and recognitions over the years from the victim and victim advocacy communities for his contributions to the field, most notably the National Organization of Victim Assistance's prestigious Edith Surgan Victim Activist of the Year award in 2006. He frequently speaks at national and regional conferences throughout the US and Canada, teaching and training victim advocates and others working in the criminal justice system.

What to Consider After Experiencing a HUSH Topic?

After experiencing a traumatic event, you may feel overwhelmed, and feel like your thoughts are consumed with the event. Below are steps that you can consider, to help you transition from Victim to Survivor.

1. Safety is the most important thing you should focus on. Consider calling 9-1-1, family member/friends, or a local advocacy agency to report the incident. Local police officers, victim advocates, and counselors can help you develop a safety plan or help you apply for a restraining order.

2. Health is also a major concern. Consider going to your local hospital for an examination. A victim advocate can accompany you to the hospital or one can be called once you get there. When you arrive at the hospital, go to the check-in desk, and tell them that you need to speak to someone in private. The hospital staff will immediately take you to the back so that you do not have to speak in front of the entire waiting room. The hospital will assign a Doctor or a Sexual Assault Nurse Examiner to examine and support you through the process. Remember that the hospital can test you for pregnancy and sexually transmitted infections, as well as collect evidence that can be used to prosecute your offender. The hospital can also give you medication to prevent pregnancy called emergency contraception (EC). This form of birth control can delay ovulation, stop fertilization of an egg,

or stop an egg from attaching. EC is not an abortion and does not end an existing pregnancy.

3. Counseling is something that victims forget about because some injuries are not seen. If you are experiencing any anxiety, sleep disturbances, increase substance use, depression, or if you are feeling suicidal, talk to your primary care doctor, counselor, or advocate. Your mental health is just as important as your physical health.

4. Healing is the ultimate step to achieve after a traumatic event. This step and timing is different for everyone. Hopefully, this book will encourage you to take the first step.

How Do I HUSH No More?:

Coming forward and sharing your truth is a hard decision because it is NOT easy. When you are ready, answer these three questions. After you have fully answered these questions, add the answers into your story as you share your truth. Remember that people may not believe you or agree with your decision. During these times, remember that You Have a Right to Tell It.

1. Who am I?
2. What have I learned?
3. What do I need to do to move forward as a Survivor?

5 Ways to Prevent Sexual Abuse:

1. Become informed about the tactics that offenders use to commit abuse.
2. If you have to keep a meeting with someone a secret, don't go. Your friends and family should always know where you are and who you are with.
3. Never trust your drinks or food around anyone. Covering it up does not protect you from being drugged. Don't let someone buy or make you a drink without you watching.
4. Say an assertive "NO" and stand your ground. Don't say "maybe" or sound unsure. Make sure you leave the situation.
5. Use your intuition. If your mind tells you not to do it, or your stomach feels queasy, pay attention. Our body has a natural safety alarm

Friends & Family Support

5 Ways to Prevent or Interrupt an Act of Violence

1. Increase awareness: Make eye contact with the victim to let them know you're aware and look for their signals. Asses the best way to step-in or if the situation is too dangerous to approach alone.

2. Distraction: Do what you can to interrupt the situation. A distraction can give someone a chance to get to a safe place. Cut off any conversation with a diversion. You can also move around physically in a way to create space that disrupts the conversation or potentially harmful behaviors.

3. Ask for help: It can be intimidating to approach a situation alone. Enlist another person to support and come with you when you approach the person at risk. You can also ask someone to intervene in your place, like a friend, bartender, or security guard.

4. Be direct: Talk directly to the person who might be in trouble. Ask questions like "Who did you come here with?" "Would you like me to stay with you?"

Once the act is under control or over, offer your support. You can be an ally by letting victims know you stand with them and finding out what they need and how can you better support them after an incident. A simple, "How are you?", "Can I do anything?", "I'm so sorry this happened." Positive words and offering your support can make a huge difference.

GIVE is a way that you can remember how to be supportive to your friends and family members when they come to you for help.

Gentle: Be gentle and courteous. Don't judge or blame.

Interested: Don't interrupt. Be patient and listen.

Validate: Acknowledge their feelings; it does not mean you agree.

Easy manner: Reassure, encourage, support, empathize, and offer soft suggestions that include safety.

After a person has experienced trauma, this is when they need you the most. Be supportive and love on them. If they distance themselves from you, don't take it personally and give them some space and time. This is a form of showing your love and support. When they are ready, they will talk to you, or they may not. Regardless, pray for them and ensure that they know that you are there for them when they are ready.

Support Hotline Numbers

Feeling overwhelmed? There are a lot of phone numbers on this page. If you don't know where to start, call 2-1-1 on your phone to be connected with the National Human Service Center or HUSH No More at 1-888-285-2161. Contact 9-1-1 for all emergencies.

Sexual Assault

National Sexual Assault Hotline 1-800-656-HOPE (4673)

DOD Safe Helpline 1-877-995-5247 (Military)

National Child Abuse Helpline 1-800-4-A-CHILD (422-4453)

Comfort In The Storm 562-547-5064

ADDICTION

Drug Abuse Helpline 1-800-662-4357

Alcoholic Anonymous 1-212-870-3400

DOMESTIC VIOLENCE

National Domestic Violence Hotline 1-800-799-SAFE (7233)

National Domestic Violence Hotline (Spanish) 1-800-942-6908

Battered Women and Their Children 1-800-603-HELP (4357)

Elder Abuse Hotline 1-800-252-8966

Family Violence Prevention Center 1-800-313-1310

Suicide

Suicide Hotline 1-800-SUICIDE (784-2433)/1-800-273-TALK (8255)

Suicide Prevention Hotline 1-800-827-7571

VA Suicide Helpline 1-855-302-6626

CHRISTIAN COUNSELING

National Prayer Line 1-800-4-PRAYER (772937)

Grace Help Line 24 HRs Christian Service 1- 800-982-8032

About the Author

Dr. Vanessa Dunn Guyton is the Founder and Executive Director of HUSH No More, a non-profit organization and movement that provides a platform to allow Survivors to share their story and help victims to heal and unleash the shame of their trauma. This platform led to her creating and producing the HUSH No More Documentary. Her documentary has been shown internationally in Japan, Kuwait, Jordan, and Qatar to bring awareness to the HUSH Topics. Additionally, she is the CEO of Consulting Experts & Associates, LLC. CEA is a global training consulting firm that assists organizations in improving training and organization effectiveness. Dr. Guyton honorably served in the United States Army as a Human Resource Specialist for ten years. Additionally, she is a credentialed Victim Advocate and has certified over 3,200 Sexual Assault Response Coordinators and Victim Advocates. Her training is provided globally to thousands of military organizations, colleges, and corporations on The Hush Topics: sexual assault, sexual harassment, drug-facilitated sexual assault, LGBTQ sexual assault, disabled victims, sex trafficking, suicide prevention, domestic violence, bystander intervention, and refresher training for Victim Advocates. She believes that awareness and knowledge lead to prevention. Dr. Guyton is the proud mother of five children, Keith, Teaira, Tony, Miata, De'Quan and a Gigi to Braylin and Jeremiah.

Follow and connect with Dr. Guyton

www.hushnomorenow.org

https://www.facebook.com/hushnomoremovement/

https://www.instagram.com/hushnomore/

www.vanessaguyton.com

https://www.facebook.com/DrVanessaGuyton/

https://www.linkedin.com/in/dr-vanessa-dunn-guyton-ba818314

www.consultingexp.com

https://www.facebook.com/TheConsultingExpert/

https://twitter.com/ConsultingX

Contributing Authors: Tammy Nobles, Geneva Dunn, Ina Smith, LeDesma Terry, Andrea' Amaker, Shakira Stewart, Eleanor Parker Smith, Tina Williams, Kathy Butler, Richard Butler, Jeremiah Anderson, and Bill Jenkins

THANK YOU for supporting Dr. Guyton & HUSH No More!!

Proceeds from the sale of this book support HUSH No More, a 501c3 nonprofit organization.

Donations are used to support Survivors and provide training around the world on

The HUSH Topics.

Made in the USA
Middletown, DE
09 November 2024